ASIAN-AMERICAN
ELECTORAL PARTICIPATION

ASIAN-AMERICAN ELECTORAL PARTICIPATION

JOHN W. LEE (EDITOR)

Novinka Books
New York

Senior Editors: Susan Boriotti and Donna Dennis
Coordinating Editor: Tatiana Shohov
Office Manager: Annette Hellinger
Graphics: Wanda Serrano
Editorial Production: Vladimir Klestov, Matthew Kozlowski and Maya Columbus
Circulation: Ave Maria Gonzalez, Vera Popovic, Luis Aviles, Melissa Diaz,
        and Jeannie Pappas
Communications and Acquisitions: Serge P. Shohov
Marketing: Cathy DeGregory

Library of Congress Cataloging-in-Publication Data

Asian-American electoral participation/ John W. Lee (editor).
     p. cm.
   Includes index
   ISBN 1-59033-515-5.
    1. Asian Americans—Politics and government. 2. Asian Americans—Suffrage. 3.
Political participation—United States. 4. Voting—United States. 5. Elections—
United States. I. Lee, John W., 1962-

E184.o6 .A8268 2002
324.7'089'95073—dc21

2002514117

Copyright © 2002 by Novinka Books, An Imprint of
        Nova Science Publishers, Inc.
        400 Oser Ave, Suite 1600
        Hauppauge, New York 11788-3619
        Tele. 631-231-7269   Fax 631-231-8175
        e-mail: Novascience@earthlink.net
        Web Site: http://www.novapublishers.com

Printed in the United States of America

CONTENTS

PREFACE

In the mid-19th century, Asian-Americans flocked to America and provided cheap immigrant labor. Their numbers grew so high and fast that several restrictive immigration laws were enacted, and were not eased until the mid-20th century. Since that time, Asian-Americans have consistently been cited as one of the fastest growing segments of the population and seem on the cusp of increased political activity and influence. Despite the rise in Asian-American citizens since the 1960s, however, there has not been a corresponding growth of political participation. Voter turnout is low, and the number of Asian-American representatives has lagged. However, Asian-Americans have often been notable political donors and campaign financiers, indicating a behind-the-scenes political influence. As the Asian population increases in the nation, so do the chances of their wielding wider impact on election results and the issues of importance nationally.

In order to understand the development of the Asian-American political bloc, this book discusses the history of Asian immigration and political participation. Using reports based on census data, the patterns of Asian-American behavior are assessed. No segment of American society can be ignored, and this book is necessary for coming to understand the implications of and history behind the political influence of a significant slice of the American pie.

Chapter 1

INTRODUCTION

Kevin Coleman

Asian immigration to the United States first began in the 1840s, climbing steadily throughout the latter half of the 19th century, until restrictive immigration policies were enacted. Thereafter, immigration from Asia dropped substantially, and at times, the number of Asians returning to their native countries outnumbered those arriving. New immigration laws adopted in 1952 and 1965 modified or removed many of the immigration restrictions, and the number of Asians arriving here has again surged since that time.

The Asian American population has grown enormously since 1960, from 900,000 people to over seven million in the 1990 Census. This constitutes just under three percent of total U.S. population, but more than 60 percent of Asian Americans live in three States: California, Hawaii, and New York. The geographical concentration (making up nearly 10 percent of California's population, for example) offers the opportunity for especially strong influence in certain States.

As one of the fastest growing segments of the population, Asian Americans are almost certain to become more active politically. This report traces what is known about Asian American political behavior and examines some of the factors that may shape participation in the future.

Section one provides an historical overview of Asian American history and a demographic profile of the population based on the 1990 Census. The second section, the main focus of this report, is devoted to Asian American participation in electoral politics. Asian Americans have been notably active as political contributors, but voting participation is rather low (for example, only 3 percent of California voters in recent years have been Asian American), as is the number of elected officials. A series of tables and figures provides information on the Asian American voting age population in selected States and congressional districts, on Federal elected officials, and on public opinion on policy issues. The report is designed to serve as a guide to understanding the emerging phenomenon of Asian American electoral participation.

Chapter 2

THE ASIAN AMERICAN POPULATION IN THE U.S.

Kevin Coleman

I. HISTORICAL OVERVIEW

The history of modern Asian immigration into the United States is one of surge, decline, and renewal. While census records establish the presence of a very small number of Asians in the United States by the turn of the 19th century, the first large scale immigration, by Chinese, began in California in the 1850s, shortly after the United States annexed vast new territories in the West. Arriving almost simultaneously with the influx of Anglo settlers generated by the California gold rush, these Chinese immigrants provided much-needed labor in the transformation of the Pacific coast from frontier to developing region. Despite cultural and ethnic differences, these early Asian arrivals were initially accepted by the dominant Anglo culture, although they were subject to informal prejudice and discrimination.

By the 1880s, however, hostility increased, and immigration policies concerning Asia grew more restrictive, eventually resulting in a virtual ban on entry from all Asian nations. Policies that controlled immigration from Asia—the Chinese Exclusion Act, the Gentleman's Agreement with Japan, and the Immigration Act of 1924—and the underlying assumptions and attitudes that were the basis for them largely determined both the magnitude of Asian settlement in the United States and the experience of immigrants once they had arrived. The McCarran-Walter Act (the Immigration and Nationality of 1952) and the 1965 amendments to it changed or ended longstanding restrictions on Asian immigration; since then, the flow of Asian immigration, interrupted nearly one hundred years before, began again. The remarkable revival of this movement, after an eight decade interruption, was largely unintended and entirely unexpected. Its effect on society—economically, culturally, and, of special interest in this report, politically—is similarly unpredictable.

Early Immigrants from Asia: The Chinese and Japanese[1]

For over a century, most Asians in the United States were of either Chinese or Japanese origin. Nearly all early immigrants were men, intending to stay long enough to accumulate the means for improving their circumstances upon returning home. Chinese laborers found work in mines and on railroads, but friction developed between the Chinese and Anglo workers once the need for manual labor declined, eventually erupting into mob violence, lynchings, and forced departures. Between 1860 and 1890, anti-Asian riots broke out in cities and remote towns scattered across the west in California, Washington, Wyoming, Colorado, and Nevada. Growing public suspicion and labor market conflict brought on by Chinese immigration, termed the "Yellow Peril" in the press, resulted in passage of the Chinese Exclusion Act of 1882, which barred entry by contract laborers for ten years, and eventually led to even more restrictive measures aimed at the immigrants. Thereafter, Chinese laborers drifted to cities where "Chinatowns" offered segregated havens from an unaccommodating society.

Japanese immigration climbed rapidly just as Chinese immigration began to fall off, and a similar scenario unfolded. Japanese laborers found work in agriculture, as Chinese immigrants had in mining and on the railroads. Though they did not suffer the hardships faced by the Chinese during the turbulent, violent period of western expansion, the familiar pattern of resistance toward Asians, now arriving from Japan, was expressed in the Gentleman's Agreement of 1908, whereby the Japanese government agreed to withhold passports from laborers bound for the United States.

Chinese immigration had peaked in the 1880s, and Japanese immigration reached its height around 1910, after which time immigration restrictions and outmigration trends often meant that more immigrants

---

[1] Note that for purposes of this paper American Indians are not included.

returned home than arrived. Thus, over a period of several decades, a pattern of reaction to Asian immigration was established: initial acceptance to meet a high demand for cheap labor; rising hostility based on the perception of the group as a disruptive, alien presence (in the labor market as well as in society at large); followed by a period during which immigration restrictions, segregation, and discriminatory practices were adopted in reaction to the perceived "foreign threat." The Immigration Act of 1924 set numerical restrictions on immigration based on the foreign born population already in the country, nearly halting the flow of immigrants from Asia.

Immigration in the Twentieth Century

The question of Asian immigration as a public issue subsided in the early years of the 20th century, once restrictive laws took effect. But the eastern hemisphere soon posed a new threat to American foreign policy interests, drawing the country into three wars over the course of as many decades in an effort to, first, contain Japanese aggression and, later, the spread of communism. These events increased public awareness of Asia and at times, demonstrated the unease that characterized long-standing attitudes toward Asian Americans and immigrants. During World War II, 121,000 persons of Japanese descent, a majority of whom were American citizens, were confined to internment camps. Following the Vietnam War, the issue of political refugees and children born to American servicemen again forced a public examination of prevailing attitudes toward Asians. With respect to immigration policy, the McCarran-Walter Act of 1952 (P.L. 82-414) lessened some restrictions on gaining citizenship and abolished the category called "alien, ineligible for citizenship" that applied to many immigrants from Asia. The legislation also created preference categories for applicants with family members in the United States and immigrants with certain skills, policies that eased the immigration process for vast numbers of Asians in the decades that followed.

Since 1965, when amendments to the Immigration and Nationality Act (P.L. 89-236) eliminated restrictions that had suppressed immigration from the Eastern Hemisphere for nearly a century, Asian immigration has increased sharply. While the Immigration Act of 1924 had strictly limited immigration from Asian countries under the national origins quota system, the new law set a limit of approximately 20,000 immigrants from each Asian country. The subsequent increase in the number of immigrants from Asian countries—particularly China, the Philippines, Vietnam, Korea, and India—

made the Asian community the fastest growing segment of the population (in percentage terms) in recent decades. According to Census counts, the Asian population grew from less than 900,000 in 1960 to just over seven million in 1990, and the trend is expected to continue well into the next century, when the Asian American population is projected to exceed 20 million.

II. POPULATION LEVELS AND SUBGROUPS

In common with European immigrants of the early 20th Century, Americans who trace their ancestry to Asia differ from one another in their history, language, religion, national origin, physical characteristics, cultural beliefs, and time of arrival in the United States. The problem in grouping all Asian ethnicities and nationalities together is similar to that in discussing the cluster of European immigrants as a single classification—the differences outnumber any similarities. Attempting to understand the Nation's diverse population by grouping people according to continent or hemisphere of origin is a common and somewhat useful practice, but many generalizations about Asian ethnics are not broadly applicable. Whether one is from Mongolia or Vietnam, Nepal or the Philippines, the less meaningful identification of "Asian" is often the only one applied, even though these groups may have as little in common as did European immigrants from Sweden and Italy a century ago. For Asian Americans in particular, such generalizing sometimes overshadows the unique heritage of each specific ethnicity or nationality, a distinction that is generally acknowledged for America's other ancestral groups.

As a way of demonstrating the wide range of ethnic and national identities that are called Asian, the Census Bureau included the following ethnic/national identifications under the broader designation of Asian and Pacific Islander in the 1990 census: Chinese, Filipino, Japanese, Asian Indian, Korean, Vietnamese, Cambodian, Hmong, Laotian, Thai, Other Asian, Hawaiian, Samoan, Guamanian, and Other Pacific Islander. In addition, the Census Bureau designated as Asian another 38 identifications provided by respondents to the question that asked for the respondent's race.[2]

---

[2] Other answers were: Bangladeshi, Bhutanese, Borneo, Burmese, Celebesian, Ceram, Indochinese, Indonesian, Iwo-Jiman, Javanese, Malayan, Maldivian, Nepali, Okinawan, Pakistani, Sikkim, Singaporan, Sri Lankan, Sumatran, Asian unspecified (Asian American, Asian, Asiatic, Amerasian, and Eurasian), Carolinian, Fijian, Kosraean, Melanesian, Micronesian, Northern Mariana Islander, Palauan, Papua New Guinean, Ponapean

In the United States, Asian Americans are by far the fastest growing segment of the population, based on percentage increase. Between the 1980 and 1990 censuses, the Asian population in the U.S. grew by 108 percent, from 3,500,000 to 7,274,000, greater than the combined rates of increase for whites (6 percent), blacks (13.2 percent), and Hispanics (53 percent) for the same period. In fact, the Asian ethnic community in America grew even faster between 1970 and 1980 (by 127.5 percent) than it did in the last decade.[3] The Asian community is now more than five times the one and a half million it was in 1970.

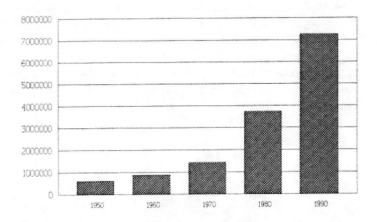

Figure 1. Asian American Population, 1950-1990

Source: (For 1950-1970:), Barringer, Herbert R., Robert W. Gardner, and Michael J. Levin. *Asians and Pacific Islanders in the United States.* NY, Russell Sage Foundation, 1993. pp. 39-41; (1980:) U.S. Department of Commerce. Bureau of the Census. *General Social and Economic Characteristics. Characteristics of the Population*, Vol. 1, Pt. 1, PC80-1-C1, December, 1983. p. 1-277; (1990:) U.S. Bureau of the Census. *General Population Characteristics. 1990 Census of Population.* 1990 CP-1-1, November, 1992. p. 3.

(Pohnpeian), Polynesian, Solomon Islander, Tahitian, Tarawa Islander, Tokelauan, Tongan, Trukese (Chuukese), Yapese, and Pacific Islander unspecified. Source: U.S. Department of Commerce. Bureau of the Census. *General Population Characteristics.* 1990 Census of Population, 1990 CP-1-1. Washington, U.S. Govt. Print. Off. 1992. p. B-12, 13.

[3] U.S. Department of Commerce. Bureau of the Census. *Race and Hispanic Origin.* 1990 Census Profile, Number 2, June 1991. pp. 1-4.

Figure 1 shows the increase in the Asian American population for post-World War II decades. As a proportion of the total U.S. population, Asian Americans were less than half a percent in 1950 and comprise just under three percent presently. The number of Asian ethnics in the United States at least doubled in each decade since the end of the Vietnam War—in the 1970s and again in the 1980's, when 2.4 million Asian immigrants entered the country.[4]

The transformation of the Asian American community over the last twenty years is chiefly the result of immigration. This surge of immigrants altered not just the size but also the composition of the Asian American population. For nearly a century and a half, Asian Americans were mostly of Japanese or Chinese ancestry. But in the short span of two decades, a massive wave of immigration from China, the Philippines and other Asian countries entirely changed the Asian community in America in nearly every respect: age, education, ancestry, economic status, etc. The mix and proportion of immigrants from "old" and "new" immigrant groups reshaped the Asian American community, and will inevitably affect its relations with the larger society.

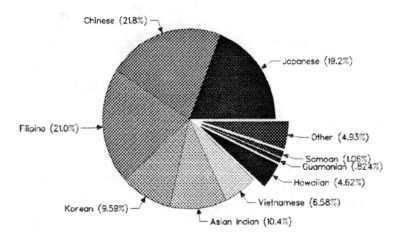

Figure 2. Asian Ethnic and National Groups in America, 1980

Source: U.S. Department of Commerce. Bureau of the Census. *Asian and Pacific Islander Population by State; 1980.* Washington, U.S. Govt. Print. Off., Dec., 1983. p. 10.

---

[4] O'Hare, William P., and Judy C. Felt. *Asian Americans: America's Fastest Growing Minority Group.* Washington, Population Reference Bureau, Inc. Number 19, February 1991. p. 2.

Chinese and Japanese comprised a fairly equal share of all Asian Americans in 1980, but Chinese immigration has grown significantly since then, while immigration from Japan continued at the same rate, creating a gap between the number of Chinese and Japanese Americans in the U.S. Between 1980 and 1990, 270,581 Chinese immigrants came to the U.S., compared with 43,248 Japanese.[5] Even more dramatic was the inflow of immigrants from the Philippines. The nearly half a million Filipinos who came constituted the largest group of immigrants from Asia in this time period.

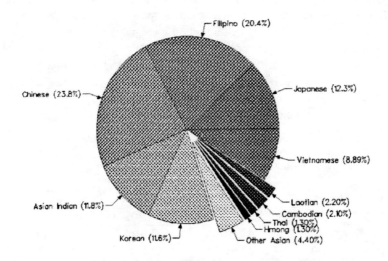

Figure 3. Asian Ethnic and National Groups in America, 1990

Source: U.S. Department of Commerce. U.S. Bureau of the Census. *We the American Asians*. Washington, U.S. Govt. Print. Off., Sept. 1993. p. 2.

Immigrants from Thailand, Vietnam, Laos, and Cambodia established comparatively large ethnic communities here almost instantly. Until the late 1960s, immigration from these Southeast Asian countries was practically nonexistent. Since then, a steady steam of immigrants—refugees as well as those emigrating for other reasons—transformed a minuscule fraction of the population into a dispersed and rapidly expanding community. Between 1956 and 1970, 10,459 immigrants from the four countries combined arrived

---

[5] Barringer, Herbert R., Robert W. Gardner, and Michael J. Levin. *Asians and Pacific Islanders in the United States*. New York, Russell Sage Foundation, 1993. p. 26.

in the U.S—less than the number of Chinese entering the country in any given year since 1965. By 1984, however, immigration from Vietnam alone was 37,236, or more than three and one half times the total for all four countries for the earlier 14 year period. Immigration from Vietnam, the country that provided by far the greatest number of arrivals from Southeast Asia, peaked at 88,543 in 1978.[6] Between 1976 and 1990, more than half a million Vietnamese entered the United States, while Laotian and Cambodian immigrants numbered 167,748 and 124,733 respectively.[7]

The flow of immigrants from China and the Philippines did not rise as sharply as did that from Southeast Asian nations, yet the number of Chinese and Filipino immigrants arriving here easily surpassed those from the "new" immigrant nations. Just under half a million immigrants from China and the Philippines arrived in this country between 1985 and 1990; Vietnam, Cambodia, Laos, and Thailand accounted for a combined immigrant total of 360,000 for the same period. Between 1971 and 1990, one and a half million persons entered the country from China and the Philippines, compared with just under one million immigrants from Southeast Asia, a difference of roughly 65 percent.

Table 1. Asian Immigration to the U.S. from 1971-1990

Country of Origin	1971-1980	1981-1990	Total
China	203,522	474,103	677,625
Hong Kong	47,501	63,016	110,517
Japan	47,914	43,248	91,162
Philippines	360,216	494,971	855,187
Korea	271,463	338,872	610,335
India	176,716	261,841	438,557
Vietnam	178,681	401,419	580,100
Cambodia	8,426	116,571	124,997
Laos	22,566	145,444	168,010
Thailand	44,055	64,437	108,492
Pakistan	31,247	61,364	92,611

Source: Barringer, et al. Asians and Pacific Islanders in the United States, p. 25, 26.

Immigrants comprise a vast segment of the Asian American population, particularly as the result of recent trends. Nearly 40 percent of these Asians arrived in the last ten years as the result of recent shifts in immigration

---

[6] Ibid., p. 25.
[7] Ibid., p. 25-26.

patterns. If all immigrants are counted, regardless of when they arrived in the United States, the proportion of Asian Americans born in another country reaches the 60 percent mark.

III. GEOGRAPHICAL DISTRIBUTION

In common with other racial and ethnic groups, Asian Americans are geographically concentrated, rather than spread evenly across the States. Whereas Europeans and Africans entered the United States by way of the East Coast, Asian immigrants landed on the Pacific Coast and, particularly during the initial period of immigration, settled and found employment almost exclusively in western States. Although the Asian population is no longer so tightly concentrated, this historical pattern is still evident today— more than 55 percent of Asians live in the western region (the Mountain and Pacific states) of the country.

Since Asian immigration to the United States began in the 1850s, California has been and remains the home for a plurality of Asian Americans (although Hawaii was the destination of large numbers of Asian immigrants long before it became a State 1959): nearly 40 percent of the total Asian population in America is found in California. New York and Hawaii rank second and third among States with the largest Asian American populations. Almost 60 percent (58.1) of the Asian population in the U.S. lives within the borders of these three States.

Within individual States, Asians accounted for 62 percent of Hawaiians and 9.6 percent of Californians in 1990. The ten States with the greatest number of Asian Americans are listed below in Table 2. Aside from Hawaii and California, the Asian population in these States constitutes from one to four percent of total population. Although Asians comprise only a small proportion of the total population in these eight States, the actual number of Asian residents is, in some cases, significantly large. In New York, for example, Asians are less than four percent of the population but number almost three quarters of a million—or more than the total population of the States of Alaska, Delaware, North Dakota, Vermont, Wyoming, and the District of Columbia. If the Asian population of California is compared with the total population of individual States, nearly half the States in the country (21) and the District of Columbia have fewer people.[8]

---

[8] These States are Alaska, Arkansas, Delaware, Iowa, Kansas, Maine, Mississippi, Montana, Nebraska, Nevada, New Hampshire, New Mexico, North Dakota, Oregon, Rhode Island, South Dakota, Utah, Vermont, and Wyoming.

Eighty percent of ethnic Asians in America live in the ten States listed in Table 2. The combined Asian American population of these States is 5,769,651, more than the population of all but the thirteen largest States.[9]

Table 2. Ten States with the Highest Asian American Populations, 1990

State	Asian Population	Total Population	Asian Percentage of the Total Population
California	2,845,659	29,760,021	9.56
New York	693,760	17,990,455	3.86
Hawaii	685,236	1,108,229	61.83
Texas	319,459	16,986,510	1.88
Illinois	285,311	11,430,602	2.50
New Jersey	272,521	7,730,188	3.53
Washington	210,958	4,866,692	4.33
Virginia	159,053	6,187,358	2.57
Florida	154,302	12,937,926	1.19
Massachusetts	143,392	6,016,425	2.38

Source: U.S. Census Bureau of the Census. 1990 Census of Population. General Population Characteristics. United States, p. 333.

Asian Americans are a highly urbanized population: ninety-four percent live in metropolitan areas. Not surprisingly, the leading metropolitan areas are (Honolulu) Hawaii, (Los Angeles-Long Beach) California and (New York City) New York. Table 3. lists the ten metropolitan areas with the greatest number of Asian American. Of the 7,274,000 Asian Americans in the United States, 3,777,000, or more than half, reside in the metropolitan areas listed in Table 3. California is home to the largest Asian American community in the country; the State contains six of the ten metropolitan areas with the highest Asian ethnic populations. The California metropolitan areas listed in the table account for nearly 85 percent of all Asian Americans living in the State. This trend holds true in other States as well. In both Illinois and New York, almost 85 percent of the Asian American population lives in a single metropolitan area, Chicago and New York City, respectively.

---

[9] The thirteen largest States in the country, ranked by population, are: California, New York, Texas, Florida, Pennsylvania, Illinois, Ohio, Michigan, New Jersey, North Carolina, Georgia, Virginia, and Massachusetts.

Table 3. Highest Asian American Populations in Metropolitan Areas*

City	Asian Population	Total Asian Population in the State	Percent of State's Asian Population in Metropolitan Area
Los Angeles-Long Beach, CA	955,000	2,710,000	35.2
New York, NY	556,000	666,843	83.4
Honolulu, HI	526,000	646,404	81.4
San Francisco, CA	330,000	2,710,000	12.2
Oakland, CA	270,000	2,710,000	10.0
San Jose, CA	261,000	2,710,000	9.6
Anaheim-Santa Ana, CA	249,000	2,710,000	9.2
Chicago, IL	230,000	275,568	83.5
Washington, D.C.	202,000	NA	NA
San Diego, CA	198,000	2,710,000	7.3

*Metropolitan areas may be comprised of several (or parts of) distinct jurisdictions. The metropolitan areas listed here do not conform to the boundaries of a single city or county, but are artificially constructed geographic areas based on population and other criteria. The Washington, D.C., metropolitan area, for example, includes jurisdictions in both Maryland and Virginia.

Source: Asian American Demographics. *The American Enterprise*, v. 2, November /December 1991. p. 88.

IV. DEMOGRAPHIC CHARACTERISTICS

The social and economic circumstances of Asian Americans are varied. Some are well-educated and affluent, while others, particularly some recent immigrants, are poor and unskilled, and struggle with the added difficulty of establishing a new life in a foreign country. Some differences are related to the length of time in the U.S., and some reflect the distinct circumstances of refugees as compared with immigrants who left their native country for other reasons. Many second and third generation Asians have attained middle class status or better as they moved beyond the "new immigrant" stage. But personal circumstances and resources vary, even among the newly arrived. Differences in education, work skills, and personal wealth at the time of arrival have further contributed to the dissimilar circumstances that exist within the Asian ethnic community.

Income

Median family income is higher for Asian Americans than it is for (non-Hispanic) whites, Hispanics, or blacks for several reasons. Family size (more persons working per family), high educational attainment, and even the highly urban character of the Asian American population contribute to pushing family incomes upward. However, individual earning is lower for Asian Americans than for whites, and the rate of poverty increased greatly as immigration climbed in the past 20-30 years. The reconfiguration of the Asian community set in motion a number of different or even conflicting trends, which make it especially difficult to generalize about social and economic circumstances. In this respect, the Asian American community has become more disparate and, therefore, more like the general population.

Family income for Asian Americans exceeds that for all other groups and underscores some of the characteristics for which they are admired by others (see the public opinion section in chapter VI). The perception that Asian Americans value close-knit families, a strong work ethic, and a high level of achievement in education and on the job appears to be supported in reality. According to the 1990 Census, the median family income of Asian Americans was $41,251, compared with $37,628 for non-Hispanic whites, $25,064 for Hispanics, and $22,429 for blacks.[10]

Asian American families are larger than the national median, and more family members are in the work force compared to other groups: in 20 percent of Asian American families, three or more family members work, compared with a national figure of 13 percent.[11] Asians are also very likely to live in urban areas, where incomes are higher (see Table 3 above). Forty percent of the total Asian American population in the country lives in California, which has one of the highest median family income nationally. California's median family income exceeds the figure for the Nation ($40,559, compared with $35,225 for the U.S.) and all but six other States.[12] The Asian population in that State is greatly concentrated in urban areas where salaries (and the cost of living) are highest, a phenomenon that holds true in other States as well. Educational attainment among Asian Americans

---

[10] U.S. Department of Commerce. Bureau of the Census. *1990 Census of Population. Social and Economic Characteristics.* 1990 CP-2-1, November 1993. p. 48.

[11] U.S. Department of Commerce. Bureau of the Census. *We the American Asians.* WE-3, September, 1993. p. 6.

[12] The six States with a higher median family income are New Hampshire ($41,628), Massachusetts ($44,367), Connecticut ($49,199), New Jersey ($47,589), Alaska ($46,581), and Hawaii ($43,176). U.S. Bureau of the Census. *1990 Census of Population. Social and Economic Characteristics*, p. 243, 247.

is notably high, particularly the large proportion of college educated persons; this factor also bears directly on earning ability.

The per capital earnings of Asian American workers, however, lags slightly behind that of whites, but is higher than blacks and Hispanics. The Census reported a median per capita income of $13,638 for Asian Americans and $15,687 for whites, while blacks and Hispanics earn just under $9,000 (according to the median Census figures).[13] While family incomes tend to create the perception that Asian Americans are thriving economically, lower personal earnings suggest more muted success. With more family members working, individual salaries are less important, but larger families also create a greater financial challenge. Also, medians do not explain the full range of circumstances: many families have fewer than three persons in the workforce; unemployment and poverty are on the rise in some segments of the Asian American community; and salaries do not necessarily reflect the characteristically strong educational qualifications of some Asian workers.

Vast income differences exist among the various Asian American groups from a per capita high of $19,373 for Japanese Americans to a low of $2,292 for Hmong (a population group from the hill country of Laos whose ancestry can be traced to China). Figures for all of the "old" Asian immigrant groups—the Japanese, Asian Indians, Chinese, Filipino, and Koreans—exceed the $10,000 threshold, while those for "new" immigrants, with the exception of Thais ($11,970), fall below that mark.

Poverty statistics starkly portray the economic polarization occurring in the Asian American community, whose overall poverty rate is 11.6 percent. While this is only slightly higher than the national average, the figure obscures the dire economic circumstances of large portions of the population, particularly Southeast Asian subgroups. The most vivid example are Hmong families, of which more than six in ten live below the poverty level. Poverty rates for Cambodian, Vietnamese, and Laotian families are also two to four times the national rate of 10 percent. More than others, including blacks and Hispanics whose family poverty rates exceed that of whites by approximately 20 percent, some immigrant families from Southeast Asia (Hmong families in particular) face extremes of poverty.[14]

---

[13] U.S. Bureau of the Census. *1990 Census of Population. Social and Economic Characteristics. United States*, p. 48.

[14] Ibid., p. 119.

Education

The emphasis Asian Americans place on attaining an education is widely recognized and admired, perhaps more than any other trait. Such admiration is well founded because Asian Americans are more highly educated than the national population. The percentage of Asian Americans who are at least high school graduates exceeds that of most groups and matches that of whites (87 percent, compared with 86 percent for whites), while college graduates and those with advanced degrees are proportionally more numerous in the Asian community than in any other group. Immigration policy has also contributed to the high education levels among Asian Americans because of the preference categories created under the 1952 Immigration Act to attract skilled and highly educated immigrants.

Nearly twice as many Asian Americans aged 25 and older have bachelor's degrees or better, compared with whites: 37 percent of these Asians attained a 4 year degree or higher, while 21 percent of the whites have done so. For each academic degree offered—bachelor's, master's and doctorate, the proportion of Asian Americans is at least double that of whites.[15] In the workforce, however, Asian Americans reportedly earn less than whites, whose educational qualifications are the same. According to a *Washington Post* article comparing education and earning, median income for Asians with four or more years of college was $34,470, while for whites, it was $36,130.[16] Asian American women and white women with four or more years of college earn the same amount, based on median income, but the median for Asian American men is approximately $4,000 less than for white men: $37,550, compared with $41,660.[17]

One possible explanation is that Asian Americans still encounter discrimination, however subtle that impedes career advancement. Opinion polls document Asian Americans' strong views about the discrimination they face at work and in the larger society, and Asian American advocacy groups also cite negative stereotypes as a reason for the education/income disparity in comparison with whites. There are other possible explanations, however. The relative youthfulness of the Asian American population may contribute to the income gap because a large share of the workforce has not yet reached peak earning years. According to the *Washington Post* article, career choice may also affect earnings, and Asians are more likely to hold professional,

---

[15] U.S. Bureau of the Census. *Social and Economic Statistics. U.S. Summary*, p. 42.

[16] Vobejda, Barbara. Asian/Pacific Islanders Trail Whites in Earning: Comparable Education Fails to Close Gap. *Washington Post*, Sept. 18, 1994. p. A3.

[17] Ibid.

scientific and technical jobs, rather than executive positions; income potential of these jobs may not be as great. Discrimination may also hold back some Asians in management careers if employers do not "promote into executive positions persons who speak English with an accent."[18]

Family Characteristics

Asian Americans hold to more traditional views and practices about family life than many other groups, according to Census Bureau statistics on marriage, divorce, and family size. The four percent divorce rate for Asians is roughly half the rate for whites (nine percent), blacks (ten percent), or Hispanics (seven percent). Asians are about as likely to be married as are whites (56 percent, compared with 58 percent for whites) and they are more likely to be married than are blacks (34 percent) and Hispanics (50 percent).[19]

The average number of persons per family ranges from 3.1 for whites to 3.9 for Hispanics; Asians fall at the high end of the scale with an average 3.8 persons in each family. Asian American children are more likely to live with both parents than are white children, according to the Census. Similarly, the proportion of Asian American households that are family households is nearly ten percent higher than for whites: 78 percent (Asian Americans), compared with 70 percent (whites).[20]

---

[18] Ibid.

[19] U.S. Department of Commerce. Bureau of the Census. *1990 General Population Characteristics. United States*, p. 47.

[20] U.S. Department of Commerce. Bureau of the Census. Public Information Office. *Hooked on Demographics for the Month Honoring Asian & Pacific Islanders*. Undated.

Chapter 3

ASIAN AMERICANS AND ELECTORAL POLITICS

Kevin Coleman

During the past 20 years, a sharp increase in the Asian American population has created a demographic shift that will continue well into the next century. Less certain is when Asian Americans will have a corresponding effect on American politics. Demographic changes, even massive ones, do not guarantee a change in the composition of the electorate, because voters are a self-selected segment of the population—a segment that includes only those who participate. Authors Mark Levy and Michael Kramer called attention to this distinction in their survey of ethnic voting: "Demographers are interested in all people... Political analysts, of necessity, are interested in voters, a group more elusive than one might think."[1] For minority groups in particular, political power may continue to be elusive when an increase in population causes profound demographic change but does not bring a corresponding change within the electorate.

The surge in the Asian American population creates a potential to affect electoral politics, although Asian Americans remain only a fraction of the electorate nationally. Even in California, where they comprise ten percent of the population, persons of Asian descent are only three percent of eligible

---

[1] Levy, Mark R., and Michael S. Kramer, *The Ethnic Factor: How America's Minorities Decide Elections.* New York, Simon and Shuster, 1972. p. 13.

voters, a difference that can mostly be attributed to the large number of non-citizens. To maximize political power in elections, eligible voters must choose to turn out on election-day; they may cast their ballots in a similar manner, or attain political leverage by forging coalitions with other groups. Political solidarity could be especially elusive for Asian Americans because the community is comprised of several distinct ethnic or national groups. A unifying identity, at least in the political sphere, has not yet emerged, and voting participation among Asian Americans as a group is low. Asian Americans are increasingly active as political contributors, but the extent and impact of such activity in elections is difficult to assess. In general, the standard measure of political participation for subgroups of the electorate is voting; this approach may need to be modified in the case of Asian Americans if voter participation remains low and political activity centers around making contributions to candidates. There are signs of increased political involvement, but widespread Asian American activism in politics is best described as a slowly emerging phenomenon.

I. THE ASIAN AMERICAN ELECTORATE

In most States, Asian Americans comprise only a small fraction of citizens and voters. Hawaii's demographics reflect its unique location and immigrant history: persons of Asian ancestry account for 62 percent of the population and 61 percent of potential voters. Outside Hawaii, Asian Americans are fewer than ten percent of voters in each of the remaining 49 States. But in smaller political jurisdictions within the States—congressional districts, State legislative districts, cities, and counties—the steep increase in population may provide opportunities for determining the outcome of some political contests.

In both statewide and local elections recently held in California, Asian Americans have comprised between two to four percent of voters. In statewide elections from 1986-1992, Asian voters were three percent of the electorate on average (see Table below). Asian American voters were four percent of all voters in both the primary and runoff mayoral elections in Los Angeles in 1992. By way of comparison, white voters comprised 68 percent of the electorate, blacks were 18 percent, and Latinos were 8 percent in the April primary; in the June runoff, Anglos comprised a slightly higher percentage of all voters (72 percent), Latino voters also increased their share of voters (10 percent), and blacks were 12 percent.[2]

Aside from jurisdictions in which Asian Americans comprise a substantial segment of potential voters, opportunities for coalition building have expanded where combined minority groups are a sizeable bloc of voters, or even a majority. Nationwide, in eight of the ten districts listed in Table 4, minority voters together constitute a majority of the electorate, while in the remaining two, California's 12th and 13th congressional districts, the minority voting age population exceeds 40 percent of all potential voters. As minority population growth continues in the future, the chances for forming multi-racial and ethnic political coalitions are certain to increase, but whether Asian Americans will enter such alliances, even among themselves, it less certain.

Table 4. Congressional Districts with the Highest Asian American Voting Age Population (VAP)

State	District	Asian American VAP	Total VAP	Asian American Percent of VAP
Hawaii	1	277,513	431,485	64.3
Hawaii	2	207,245	396,618	52.3
California	8	122,930	481,160	26.0
California	31	95,194	403,689	24.0
California	12	106,840	455,454	24.0
California	30	86,782	415,463	21.0
New York	12	84,592	417,930	20.2
California	16	81,056	409,054	20.0
California	13	75,883	426,316	18.0
California	9	65,112	446,911	15.0

Source: Brace, Kimball W. and Election Data Services. *The Election Data Book: A Statistical Portrait of Voting in America.* Lanham, MD, Bernan Press, 1993, and unpublished information provided by Election Data Services.

The highest percentage of Asian American voters in any congressional district outside Hawaii is the 8th district of California, where they make up 26 percent of those eligible to vote. In 56 congressional districts, mostly in California, Asians are at least five percent of eligible voters. Table 5 lists these districts and shows the combined minority population in each, which

---

[2] Simon, Richard. Anglo Vote Carried Riordan to Victory. *Los Angeles Times*, June 10, 1993. p. B3.

ranges from 16 to 83 percent of the total voting age population. Given the slow rate of growth for the white population as compared to minorities, this sample of congressional districts may illustrate a future trend wherein the combined minority groups are a significant proportion and occasionally the majority, of constituents. In California, for example, Asian American population is projected to increase by more than 100 percent (from 3.5 to 9.7 million) by 2020, dramatically affecting the demographics of some of the State's congressional districts.[3] The average minority proportion of the voting age population in these 56 districts is 36 percent, and the average Asian American percentage is 11.5 percent.

Table 5 only includes districts arbitrarily chosen on the basis of the Asian population; consequently, other districts with a high concentration of minority voters (including those in which the Asian American population is less than five percent) are not listed. Even under the limitations imposed for compiling this selected list, 13 of the districts in Table 5 have a combined minority population that is 50 percent or higher.

II ATTITUDES TOWARD PUBLIC ISSUES: SURVEY RESEARCH FINDINGS

Few opinion polls reporting Asian Americans' views on public issues are available. Most likely, this is because the community is comparatively small, includes a sizeable number of non-citizens, and grew to its present size of three percent of the total population only recently. Polltakers do not often focus on smaller segments of the population because finding an adequate sample of a small group requires intensive effort. Polls tend to gauge opinions in the broadest sense rather than precisely—questions are often phrased to reveal only general agreement or disagreement on an issue—an approach that guide selection of the sample as well. In the future, as the Asian ethnic population grows, polling organizations will likely increase their efforts to solicit the views of Asian Americans.

---

[3] U.S. Department of Commerce. Bureau of the Census. Press Release, Apr. 22, 1994. p. 2.

Table 5. Congressional Districts in Which Asian Americans Comprise Five Percent or More of the Voting Age Population

State and CD	Asian	Black	Hispan	Native Amer.	Total Minority VAP	White
California 3	5.2	2.8	12.0	1.1	21.1	78.7
California 5	11.4	10.9	12.7	0.9	35.9	63.9
California 7	12.7	14.9	11.7	0.6	39.9	59.8
California 8	25.5	11.1	14.1	0.4	51.1	48.7
California 9	14.6	28.5	10.7	0.5	54.3	45.6
California 10	5.7	2.1	7.8	0.5	16.1	83.7
California 11	9.1	4.9	19.0	0.8	33.8	66.1
California 12	23.5	3.8	12.8	0.3	40.4	59.5
California 13	17.8	6.6	16.6	0.6	41.6	58.3
California 14	11.2	4.3	11.7	0.3	27.5	72.3
California 15	10.3	1.9	9.7	0.4	22.3	77.5
California 16	19.8	4.7	33.4	0.5	58.4	41.3
California 17	5.8	4.1	26.8	0.6	37.3	62.5
California 19	5.4	2.7	20.5	1.0	29.6	70.2
California 24	5.9	1.8	12.0	0.3	20.0	79.9
California 25	6.1	4.0	14.9	0.5	25.5	74.4
California 26	7.1	5.5	46.9	0.4	59.5	39.9
California 27	9.7	7.2	18.4	0.4	35.7	64.3
California 28	11.9	4.9	21.3	0.4	38.5	61.4
California 29	7.2	3.2	11.7	0.3	22.4	77.4
California 30	20.9	3.2	57.1	0.3	81.5	18.2
California 31	23.6	1.5	53.8	0.3	79.2	20.7
California 34	9.0	1.6	58.1	0.3	69.0	30.7
California 36	11.3	2.8	13.1	0.4	27.6	72.4
California 38	7.8	6.6	21.9	0.5	36.8	63.1
California 39	12.6	2.3	20.3	0.4	35.6	64.4
California 41	9.5	6.1	28.5	0.4	44.5	55.2
California 45	9.7	1.1	13.1	0.4	24.3	75.7
California 46	11.5	2.2	45.3	0.3	59.3	40.5
California 47	8.8	1.6	11.7	0.3	22.4	77.5
California 49	5.6	4.7	11.2	0.5	22.0	77.9
California 50	13.3	13.1	36.4	0.5	63.3	36.5
California 51	7.4	1.5	12.1	0.4	21.4	78.5

California 52	2.7	2.6	19.4	0.9	25.6	74.3
Hawaii 1	64.3	2.2	4.7	0.3	71.5	28.4
Hawaii 2	52.3	2.2	7.6	0.4	62.5	37.3
Illinois 5	5.1	1.3	11.0	0.2	17.6	82.3
Illinois 9	8.9	10.3	8.4	0.3	27.9	72.0
Maryland 8	7.5	7.3	6.0	0.2	21.0	79.0
Massachusetts 8	5.4	18.8	9.0	0.2	33.4	66.1
New Jersey 9	5.7	5.7	10.5	0.1	22.0	77.9
New York 5	9.5	3.0	6.8	0	19.3	80.5
New York 6	5.9	51.8	6.8	0.6	65.1	25.5
New York 7	10.6	8.1	19.6	0.2	38.5	61.2
New York 8	6.0	6.6	11.5	0.2	24.3	75.6
New York 9	5.8	2.7	7.7	0.1	16.3	83.6
New York 12	20.2	8.3	54.3	0.2	83.0	16.5
New York 13	5.0	4.3	6.6	0.1	16.0	83.8
New York 14	5.2	3.7	9.7	0.1	18.7	81.1
New York 18	7.3	6.5	9.7	0.1	23.6	76.3
Texas 7	5.0	5.1	10.9	0.2	21.2	78.7
Texas 22	6.4	7.2	14.4	0.3	28.3	71.7
Virginia 8	6.0	12.2	8.0	0.3	26.5	73.4
Virginia 11	7.6	7.3	7.0	0.2	22.1	77.8
Washington 7	10.4	8.3	3.1	1.2	23.0	77.1
Washington 9	5.3	4.6	3.1	1.2	14.2	85.6

Source: Brace, Kimball W. and Election Data Services. *The Election Data Book: A Statistical Portrait of Voting in America.* Lanham, MD, Bernan Press, 1993.

The polls and other information included here are limited to what was available through an extensive search of literature on Asian Americans, the public opinion polls files of the Congressional Research Service, and standard sources for opinion polls. The lack of detailed information prohibits forming an in-depth understanding of Asian Americans' attitudes and opinions, but may provide a guide to general perceptions held by and about members of the community.

A *San Francisco Chronicle* exit poll from the 1992 election surveyed Asian Americans' views on the political parties and the most important public policy issue, as they left 85 voting places in the Bay Area. Described by that newspaper as "the most comprehensive exit poll of Asian and Pacific Islander Americans," its results resembled national poll results for the entire electorate, differing mostly on the degree of importance these Asian voters attached to specific issues, rather than which issues they felt were most important.[4] In a similarly extensive national exit poll among all people, nearly a majority of respondents cited the economy and jobs as the most important issue.[5] The issue was even more significant to Asian Americans in the 1992 *Chronicle* poll, nearly 60 percent of whom cited it as the most important issue.

Which party cares most about needs of Asian/Pacific Americans?

Most

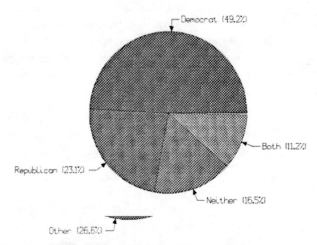

Source: *San Francisco Chronicle* exit poll, Nov. 3, 1992

Other areas of public policy, such as the deficit (3.4 percent), education (4.3 percent), health care (2.7 percent), crime and drugs (2.3 percent), and abortion (1.1 percent) were of less concern to Asian ethnic voters than to the electorate as a whole, although this may have been due to a difference in the design of the questionnaires. Asian American voters were asked to identify the most important issue, whereas voters who participated in the national survey were asked for the one or two issues that mattered most to them. Twenty-two percent of the Asian voters interviewed named an issue other

[4] Chung, L.A. Asian Americans Backed Clinton. *San Francisco Chronicle*, Nov. 6, 1992. p 1. Nearly 2,000 voters were questioned as they left polling places in San Francisco, Daly City, Oakland, Union City, Fremont, and Hayward; a sample of approximately 1,000 persons is considered viable.

[5] Voter Research and Surveys, December, 1992. The survey was based on 15,490 interviews with voters as they left polling places on election day.

than the above-mentioned ones. Voters in the national survey ranked other issues besides the economy as follows: health care (20 percent), the deficit (21 percent), abortion (12 percent), education (13 percent), the environment (5 percent), taxes (14 percent), foreign policy (8 percent), and family values (15 percent).

A second question in the 1992 *Chronicle* poll asked Asian ethnic voters to identify which political party "cares the most about the needs of Asian/Pacific Americans?" Nearly a majority named the Democratic Party, while one-fourth of respondents identified the Republican Party. Since the question asked for perceptions of the parties rather than the voter's specific party identification, the results are not comparable to the party affiliation question asked in the national survey. In fact, when Asian Americans were asked about their party identification in a separate national poll in late 1992, they split evenly among the two political parties and the independent label (see the section on party preference in the chapter on electoral participation, p. 34).

Which party cares most about needs of Asian/Pacific Americans?

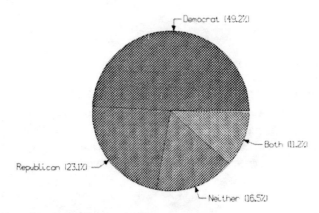

Source: *San Francisco Chronicle* exit poll, Nov. 3, 1992

A national exit poll from the 1992 election included a question on abortion that affords a comparison of Asian Americans' responses with those of other groups on a central public issue.[6] Compared with whites, blacks, and Hispanics, fewer Asian Americans agreed that abortion should be legal in all cases, and nearly the same percentage of Asians and Hispanics believed that abortion should be illegal in most or all cases. A series of policy questions would have permitted placing this issue in larger context and attempting to draw conclusions about how groups differ in their views. Whether the comparatively conservative response of Asian Americans to the abortion question would be consistent on other social issues is unknown; on this specific issue, however, Asian Americans are among the most conservative of groups, based on the reported results.

Which Comes Close to Your Position? Abortion Should be…

	Legal in all cases	Legal in most cases	Illegal in most cases	Illegal in all cases
Asian	22%	30%	27%	13%
White	34	30	24	9
Black	38	29	17	9
Hispanic	31	26	25	16

Source: Voter Research & Surveys, Nov. 3, 1992, in *The American Enterprise*, v. 4. January/February 1993. p. 103.

Understanding how Asian Americans view themselves within society and how they are viewed by others can be discovered, in part, by examining opinion poll results. The National Conference of Christians and Jews recently conducted a survey that explored attitudes and perceptions among various ethnic, religious, and racial groups.[7] It sought to examine beliefs and inter-group relations from several perspectives—those held by minorities regarding whites, those held by whites concerning minorities, and those of different minorities toward each other. The survey found evidence supporting the notion of a fractious American society, but it also revealed that some assumptions about inter-group friction are inaccurate or misunderstood. Minorities were more likely to view other members of minority groups negatively than were whites, for example, and white respondents largely reject the idea that minority progress is checked by a fundamentally unfair society.

---

[6] Voter Research and Surveys (which provides exit polling in national elections for ABC, CBS, CNN, and NBC News), Nov. 3, 1992.

[7] The National Conference of Christians and Jews. *Taking America's Pulse: A Summary Report of the National Conference Survey On Inter-Group Relations*. Mar. 2, 1994.

Non-Asians views about Asian Americans were mostly positive, but some ascribed characteristics or qualities were perceived as negative. Eighty-one percent of members of other groups admire and respect Asian Americans for their high professional and intellectual achievement and an even greater number (86 percent) admire their respect for elders and strong family relations.[8] Less flattering was the perception of approximately one-third of respondents that members of the Asian community are distrustful of non-Asians and believe themselves superior to others.

The results from questions concerning equal opportunity showed considerable differences in the way whites and minorities view this subject and contemporary society. The poll asked respondents to consider whether equal opportunities exist for minorities in several areas of public life, including education, the work force, the justice system, housing, and financial institutions. On four of nine such questions, more Asian Americans than whites believed that opportunities are the same for the two groups: quality of education, availability of decent housing, credit loans and mortgages, and equal justice under the law. Disagreement was found on questions related to work, police treatment, and the portrayal of Asians in the media.

Nearly half of whites believed that equal opportunities for promotion into managerial jobs exist for Asians, but fewer than 30 percent of Asian respondents agreed. More than 60 percent of whites perceived opportunities to be equal for receiving the same pay for the same job, while only about 25 percent of Asian Americans believed that to be true. Less of a difference of opinion was found on the question concerning fair treatment by police: about half of whites felt the situation is equal, and slightly more than 40 percent of Asians agreed. On the issue of whether Asians are portrayed fairly by the media, there was less than a five percent difference between white and Asian respondents, with more whites tending to believe that the media is unbiased in its portrayal of Asian Americans.

On the whole, the views and opinions of Asian Americans are not known in detail. The perceptions of other racial and ethnic groups toward Asians are generally positive, based on the National Conference of Christians and Jews poll included here, and acknowledge the strong family ties, respect for elders, and high educational and professional achievement that characterize the Asian community. While it is clear that Asian Americans believe they are subject to forms of discrimination in some areas (on the job, in the media, and by the police generally), they do not feel this is

---

[8] Ibid, p. B-9.

true with regard to educational opportunities, banks, or housing. The only public policy issue included here that allows for comparison between Asians and other groups—abortion—shows Asians to be more conservative than many others. Whether Asian Americans are socially conservative in general cannot be deduced from their response on a single policy question.

III. COALITION BUILDING AND A UNIFIED AGENDA

Creating a voting coalition of Asian Americans is the first step to promoting greater political involvement and strength, according to traditional notions about the dynamics of group politics. While similarities exist among Asian ethnic groups, assembling a voting bloc is a matter of basic political organizing because such coalitions rarely occur naturally in electoral politics. Links among different ethnic groups may appear obvious, yet the essential task of effective electoral participation—voter turnout—is a matter of sustained organizing effort. Asian ethnic groups may not coalesce easily, given differences in culture, language, and economic status. Historical animosities between certain groups are likely to divide, rather than unify, Asian-Americans. Even so, several forces outside and within the community might facilitate creation of a unified agenda and encourage voting participation.

Violence directed at Asians appears to have grown as immigration to the U.S. increased in the past 20 years. No comprehensive statistics are available on the number of hate crimes directed at Asian Americans, but many observers have noted with alarm the rise of such attacks. In some places, "Asian Americans suffer a higher per capita rate of hate crimes than any other racial minority."[9] Various motives have been ascribed to attacks on Asians. Resentment of international competition from Asia, the success of neighborhood storeowners in inner cities, and lingering hostility concerning the bombing of Pearl Harbor have been cited as explanations for Asian-targeted violence. The quest for political power may unite Asian Americans, but author Yen Le Espiritu points out that "[w]hile political benefits certainly promote pan-Asian organization, it is anti-Asian violence that has drawn the largest pan-Asian support."[10]

---

[9] Harvard Law Review. Racial Violence Against Asian Americans, v. 106. June 1993. p. 1928-29.

[10] Espiritu, Yen Le. *Asian American Panethnicity: Bridging Institutions and Identities.* Philadelphia, Temple University Press, 1992. p. 134.

Probably more than anyone else, Asian Americans themselves are aware of the rapid growth of their community. Such an awareness will almost certainly politicize the community, given the realities of living in a pluralistic society where groups compete in order to pursue their best interests. Anti-Asian discrimination, for example, encourages both the development of group consciousness and the resulting need for political activism. Party recruiting efforts also promote political awareness, and disparate levels of economic achievement that prevail in the Asian American community may have a dual effect on political awareness and activity. Community ties grow stronger with increased financial security—property owners pay attention to tax issues, parents interact with teachers and school systems, and neighborhood residents become concerned with crime, public services, zoning laws, and development issues—and a fair portion of Asian Americans are financially secure or well-off. A sense of community traditionally results in increased political participation. At the other end of the economic spectrum, contact with government agencies and services may have a politicizing affect on the poor. Immigrants who encounter government-sponsored programs at some level (Federal, state, and local) may be less inclined to avoid all forms of citizen involvement in politics and government.

Increased political activity among Asian Americans may occur independently of the development of a group approach to politics, at least in part because the very term "Asian American" is less meaningful to Americans of Asian descent than to non-Asians. Asians may simply become more active participants in politics as individuals, whether through increased contributions to candidates and higher voting turnout, or efforts to shape public policies, without any measurable or significant increase in group solidarity. An assumption that increased political activity in the future will occur only in connection with the group dynamic could be entirely incorrect and may actually complicate an understanding of how the population has become politicized. It is possible, and perhaps even likely, that rather than exhibiting greater group consciousness, Asian Americans will perceive their political interests (local or national) more in economic terms; their voting patterns may be better understood in terms of economic groupings. For instance, the voting habits of those living in wealthy suburban neighborhoods may more closely resemble their neighbors' than those of other Asian Americans, a pattern that may hold true across the economic spectrum. At a time when party labels reportedly mean less, the notion that Asian Americans will develop a strong group focus in political matters and vote as a bloc in elections is uncertain.

IV. POLITICAL PARTICIPATION

Factors Concerning Political Participation

Voter interest and participation among Asian Americans is complicated by a series of factors related to immigration and the diversity of the Asian community in the U.S. Nearly 70 percent of Asian Americans were born outside the U.S.; those who are not yet citizens are not eligible to vote. While Asians "generally naturalize to a greater extent and faster than immigrants from other parts of the world," the procedure takes time.[11] Immigrants are eligible to begin the citizenship process only after five years of residence in the United States. Between 1970 and 1979, 55.4 percent of Asian who immigrated during that time became citizens (instead of retaining "permanent resident alien" status), followed by African immigrants, the next highest group, of whom 42.7 percent had been naturalized.[12] Efforts to transform the population gain into political power must account for this naturalization step, which inevitably slows attaining increased political power.

Disparate Origins

Among some immigrants who are citizens, an attitude of distrust or fear of political involvement carried over from their home countries may discourage participation. As one observer points out, for many Asian immigrants "involvement in politics was not a safe pastime, or even an imaginable one."[13] Lacking any personal experience with open participation, many immigrants may simply avoid political involvement in any form. On the other hand, if there is political interest, it may concern only the political situation in the country from which they emigrated. Preoccupation with native country politics may divide, rather than unify, potential voters from the same country, particularly if the political situation there is volatile. This polarizing effect is especially evident among Asian Americans with ties to China, the Philippines, Korea, India, and Vietnam, and reportedly it has erupted into violence on occasion.[14] As for the prospect of cross-national Asian unity, author Yen Le Espiritu notes that "... homeland politics rarely

---

[11] Barringer, Gardner, and Levin, Asians and Pacific Islanders in the United States, p. 46.

[12] Ibid.

[13] Gurwitt, Rob. *Have Asian Americans Arrived Politically? Not Quite.* Governing, v. 4, November, 1990. p. 35.

[14] Espiritu, Yen Le. *Asian American Panethnicity: Bridging Institutions and Identities.* Philadelphia, Temple University Press, 1992. p. 60.

generates pan-Asian solidarity. Coming from different homelands, Asian immigrant groups share no foreign policy interests."[15]

Language Proficiency

Immigrants who do not speak or understand English or do so only with difficulty face numerous limitations in society at large, a problem that probably looms even larger when it involves an "official" exercise such as voting. Bilingual ballot laws are designed to eliminate language barriers to voting (P.L. 94-73) and the Voting Rights Act Extension of 1992 increased the number of jurisdictions in which bilingual voting materials are available, but the program may strain local election budgets and it does not guarantee that different-language ballots are available on election day for everyone who might require them. Los Angeles spent $125,250 in 1992 to prepare ballots in Spanish, Chinese, Japanese, Vietnamese, Tagalog, and Korean, and the county asked for nearly $300,000 in addition for the 1993 municipal elections.[16] Preparing bilingual materials can be costly, particularly in smaller jurisdictions like Long Beach, California, which spent $281.81 per voter in 1992 when 22 bilingual ballots were requested on election day. Aside from cost issues, the formula for determining whether ballots should be prepared in languages other than English depends on county populations; cities with a significant language minority may not prepare bilingual materials if the minority does not meet the county threshold.

Youth

Because many recent immigrants have been young, Asian Americans are now a comparatively youthful population, which may also hold down the overall level of participation. Turnout is traditionally lowest among younger voters, and the median age of Asian Americans is 30 years, lower than the national median of 33 years.[17] For immigrants, the median age is even lower. In the 1992 Presidential election, turnout among 18 to 30 years old ranged from 37 to 50 percent. In general, voters turn out at successively higher rates according to their age: voting is higher among people in their fifties than those in their thirties, and so on. Seventy percent of all persons 65 and older voted in 1992, fully 20 percent higher than peak turnout among the 18 to 30

---

[15] Ibid. p. 60.

[16] Gurwitt, Bob. *How Do You Say 'Party Ticket' in Tagalog?* Governing, v. 6, April, 1993. p. 26.

[17] U.S. Department of Commerce. Bureau of the Census. *We the American Asians*, p. 3.

years old.[18] If the relationship between age and voting holds true for Asian Americans who are now between 18 and 30 years old, the oldest members of the group would not reach the 70 percent level of participation until 2024. Younger members of this cohort would not reach the 70 percent plateau until 2044 and later.[19]

Alternately, the youthfulness of the Asian American population could prove an advantage over time. As the "baby boom" generation ages and the number of Americans between ages 18 and 40 shrinks, Asian Americans will comprise a larger share of that age group than presently, and they could potentially increase their political leverage as a result. Likewise, the large number of immigrants could offset traditional youthful disinterest in politics if the naturalization process produces strong civic-mindedness among the new citizens, regardless of their age.

Countervailing Factors

Despite factors that may hold down Asian American voting participation, a number of countervailing factors suggest that political activity could be on the rise. As immigrants become more familiar with American society in general and the electoral system in particular, psychological barriers to voting may lessen over time. Language difficulties are likely to decline as well, at least for those who regularly come in contact with the English speaking culture. Bilingual ballot procedures make voting easier for non-English speakers in covered jurisdictions and could help with get-out-the-vote efforts in Asian American communities. The rising number of Asian American candidates for political office may also encourage greater participation by Asian Americans, and even non-Asians seeking office are likely to focus more attention on the country's growing Asian American constituencies.

In a strictly political sense, both major political parties are reportedly making efforts to attract Asian American voters. A 1990 article on growing Asian American political activity noted that, "Democrats and Republicans are scrambling over each other to persuade Asian Americans that they can best do what they want to do within the ranks of their respective parties."[20]

---

[18] U.S. Department of Commerce. Bureau of the Census. Current Population Reports. *Voting and Registration in the Election of November 1992.* P20-466. Washington, U.S. Govt. Print. Off. April 1993. p. 1.

[19] Ibid, p. 3. The median age is lowest for recent immigrants: 13 years for Hmong, 25 years for Vietnamese, and approximately 20 years for Cambodians and Laotians. For Japanese Americans, a group with relatively few recent immigrants, the median age is 36 years.

[20] Awanohara, Susumu. Spicier Melting Pot. *Far Eastern Economic Review*, v. 50, Nov. 22, 1990. p. 32.

This attention from both parties may help Asians avoid the limitations of one-party politics, which could increase their overall effectiveness in political affairs as a result. Furthermore, bipartisan efforts to target Asian voters may be especially advantageous at this formative stage, when political sensibility is emerging.

Party efforts to recruit Asians could have the opposite effect, however, reducing their overall political leverage if divided party allegiance becomes the pattern of Asian American voters. The result would splinter the Asian American vote, thereby disrupting the possible emergence of a unified Asian American electorate. Coalition building within the Asian American community may become more difficult as the result of Democratic and Republican Party efforts to recruit specific Asian ethnic groups.

Voter Turnout

Levels of voter participation for Asian Americans over time are difficult to ascertain, but available information *suggests* that their participation is lower than for both whites and other minorities. It is likely that among Asian Americans, voting participation is lowest for recent immigrants. There is historical evidence showing that native-born citizens go to the polls more consistently than those born abroad. In *Who Voted: The Dynamics of Electoral Turnout, 1870-1980*, the author found that "the occurrence of a large gap between native-stock and foreign-born turnout is not surprising, and particularly not if we take into account the obstacles to participation that immigrants confronted—relative recency of arrival, lack of prior familiarity and experience with the electoral process, and language barriers."[21] Of course, immigrants who are not citizens cannot vote, and turnout figures are calculated on the basis of eligible voters. Consequently, noncitizens do not deflate voter turnout figures for the Asian American community.

While turnout is higher generally for whites than for minority voters, a variety of factors determine the number of voters who go to the polls on election day. Particular issues or candidates may encourage or discourage turnout, while organizational efforts before election day can reinforce the importance of casting a ballot, as well as commitments to particular candidates. Especially in primary elections where turnout is traditionally lighter, minority voters can boost their influence with strong participation,

---

[21] Kleppner, Paul. *Who Voted? The Dynamics of Electoral Turnout, 1870-1980*. New York, Praeger Publishers. 1982. p. 38.

while effective coalitions further increase the electoral strength of minority groups beyond what could be achieved by any single group on its own.

Exit poll information from the 1992 Presidential election showed Asian voters constituted one percent of all those who cast ballots in the election.[22] Comparable data on Asian voters were not collected in previous years. In 1992, the Census Bureau found that 27.3 percent of eligible Asian American voters reported going to the polls, a lower rate of participation than was reported by whites (64 percent), blacks (54 percent), or Hispanics (29 percent).

Table 6. Registration and Voting in the 1992 Presidential Election

Race and Hispanic Origin	Percent Who Reported Registered	Percent Who Reported Voting
Asian	31.2	27.3
Hispanic	35.0	28.9
Black	63.9	54.0
White	70.1	63.6

Source: U.S. Department of Commerce. Bureau of the Census. *Voting and Registration in the Election of November 1992*. P20-466. April, 1992. pps. v-vi, 71.

The *San Francisco Chronicle's* election day poll of Asian American voters in November 1992 asked a series of questions concerning registration and how these voters gathered information about the election. Nearly 74 percent of those surveyed had registered with either a volunteer on the street (39.8 percent) or at a government office other than the Naturalization Service (34.1 percent). The remaining group of voters registered through the Naturalization Service (12.2 percent) or by some other means (13.9).

Asian American voters used multiple sources to learn about the election. The great majority of persons interviewed said they learned about the election through the media (TV news, newspapers, radio news, and TV ads); television news was the most-cited source of information (67 percent of voters relied on it). Fifty-five percent reported gathering information from newspaper stories, half cited TV ads, and half relied on radio news. Each of the following sources was used by fewer than 50 percent of those interviewed: ballot pamphlets (43.4 percent), campaign mail (38.6), friends/relatives (30), radio ads (24.4), and slate cards (11).

---

[22] Voters Research and Surveys poll, *The Polling Report*. November 18, 1992. vol. 8, no. 21. p. 1.

POLITICAL CONTRIBUTIONS

In the area of political campaign contributions, Asian Americans have clearly established their presence. A number of commentators have noted that Asian Americans give money to political candidates at a rate that far exceeds what might be expected for such a small proportion of the electorate. In national politics, an "unprecedented $1.5 to 2 million" was raised by mid-September 1992 to support the Bush/Quayle campaign in the Asian American community, while the Clinton/Gore campaign raised $250,000 at a single dinner for Asian Americans in Monterey Park, California, a city with a majority Asian ethnic population.[23] In the 1988 election year, the Democratic Senatorial Campaign Committee (DSCC) collected $1.2 million for Democratic candidates through its Pacific Leadership Council, an affiliate of the DSCC that focuses on pan-Asian issues.[24]

There are also scattered examples of Asian Americans' increased activity in making contributions to candidates for office, particularly Asian American candidates. When Los Angeles City Council member Michael Woo ran to succeed Mayor Thomas Bradley in 1993, his efforts reportedly "relied in large part on the financial backing of Asian Americans from around the country who hope to make him the first big-city mayor of Asian descent."[25] And one observer estimates that in a number of recent electoral races from Delaware to California that included Asian American candidates, between 36-75 percent of all contributions came from the Asian American community.[26] Contributors from the same ethnic background as the candidate often predominate, but the pool of contributors usually includes Asian Americans from all ethnic backgrounds. In Michael Woo's (Chinese American) 1985 campaign for city council, Chinese Americans were 37 percent of contributors, and those of other Asian descent comprised 14 percent of contributors, for a combined total of $136,380. Woo's opponent in the race received $1,300 from twelve Asian American contributors.[27]

---

[23] Susumu, Awanohara and Jonathan Burton. More Money Than Votes. *Far Eastern Economic Review*, V. 155, October 29, 1992, p. 52.

[24] Espiritu, Yen Le, *Asian American Panethnicity*. p. 62.

[25] Rainey, James, and Greg Krikorian. Voters to Decide Wide Range of Choices Today. *Los Angeles Times*, June 8, 1993. p. B1.

[26] Espiritu, Asian American Panethnicity, pps. 63-65.

[27] Ibid., p. 64.

V. POLITICAL BEHAVIOR

Voting Patterns

In exit polls conducted on election-day 1992, 32 percent of Asian American voters identified themselves as Democrats, 33 percent as Republicans, and 35 percent as Independents.[28] This response matched the distribution for all respondents more closely than did other groups' responses; either Democratic or Republican party identification was stronger by about ten percent for most other groups surveyed, as compared to Asian Americans. Strong partisanship was particularly evident among blacks and Hispanics, most of whom identified themselves as Democrats, while only 8 and 9 percent respectively called themselves Republicans. The largest share of white Catholics and white Protestants identified themselves as Republicans, while a large majority of Jews claimed Democratic party identification.

Candidate preference among Asian ethnic voters, however, is a more important factor influencing their vote than their self-described party identification would suggest, although this is also true for the electorate at large. In the 1992 Presidential election, 55 percent voted to reelect President Bush, 29 percent voted for Governor Clinton and 16 percent voted for Ross Perot, based on a national poll conducted by Voter Research and Surveys (VRS).[29] A *Los Angeles Times* national exit poll, however, gave this breakdown of the Asian vote: 43 percent (Clinton), 40 percent (Bush), and 17 percent (Perot). The reason for the difference in the two polls might be a higher standard margin of error for smaller groups within the electorate, due to small sample size. This discussion relies on the Voter Research & Surveys poll because its sample size was larger by approximately 1,000 voters than the *LA Times* sample and also because the poll was the source for ABC, CBS, NBC and CNN in the 1992 election. White voters were the only other racial/ethnic group to favor President Bush, according to the Voter Research Surveys poll, although the margin between the President and Governor Clinton was much closer among that group of voters: 41 percent (Bush) to 39 percent (Clinton); Perot received 20 percent of the white vote. Blacks and Hispanics strongly favored Clinton, giving him 82 percent and 62 percent of their votes, respectively. Blacks gave Ross Perot the lowest vote of all

---

[28] Public Opinion and Demographic Report. *The American Enterprise, v 4*. January/February 1993. p. 92.

racial/ethnic groups—7 percent, while 14 percent of Hispanics cast ballots for him.[30] Asian ethnic voters supported the incumbent President much more strongly than other groups, based on the VRS poll, and as a consequence, their vote deviated more from national totals than that of other groups.

National figures for Asian ethnic voting patterns in prior years are not available from standard sources, exit polls, or Census Bureau reports on registration and voting. The table below includes exit polling data for Asian voters in California elections from 1986 to 1992. Nearly forty percent of all Asians in the United States reside in California, although recent patterns in this State contradict some noted trends for Asian voters nationally. In seven of the eight California elections surveyed, including the Presidential elections of 1988 and 1992, Asian voters in California cast most of their ballots for the Democratic candidate. The conflict in exit poll results notwithstanding, Asian Americans nationally voted strongly for President Bush in the 1992 election according to VRS results, but Asian Californians gave 45 percent of their votes to Governor Clinton and 40 percent to Bush. According to Susumu Awanohara in an article about Asian American political involvement, Asian ethnics "tend to support incumbents of whichever party," but this sample of Asian American voting patterns in California does not support that conclusion.[31] Only in two of the five races that included an incumbent (the 1986 Senatorial and Gubernatorial elections) did Asian voters cast more ballots for the incumbent office holder; one was a Democrat and one was a Republican.

In the California elections summarized in Table 7, Asian ethnic voters accounted for two percent of all those voting in 1986, four percent in 1988, and three percent in 1992. (Asian Americans presently account for three percent of eligible voters in California.) The *Los Angeles Times* exit poll of voters in 1990 did not indicate the percentage of the electorate each group comprised in that election.

---

[29] Voter Research & Surveys poll from election day in *The Polling Report*. November 16, 1992.
    p. 1.
[30] The Polling Report, November 16, 1992, p. 1.
[31] Awanohara, Spicier Melting Pot, p. 32.

Table 7. Asian American Voting in California
Statewide Elections, 1986-1992

Year	President		Senator		Governor	
	Dem	Rep	Dem	Rep	Dem	Rep
1992	45	40*	62	36*		
			51	44		
1990					52	44
1988	52	47	51	47*		
1986			56*	41	39	59*

Source: 1992 and 1990 statistics are from the *Los Angeles Times*, November 5, 1992, p.
    A14 and November 7, 1990, p. A24; 1988 and 1986 figures are from the Field
    Institute, *Voting in the 1988 General Election*, December, 1988, p. 2, and *A Survey of
    the 1986 General Election Voters*, December, 1986, p. 1.
*Denotes incumbent.

Awanohara also summarized differences of party preference among
various Asian ethnic groups in her article, noting that "Japanese and
Filipinos have been predominantly Democratic, while Korean and
Vietnamese, for ideological reasons, have gone largely Republican. In
between, Indian Americans lean more towards the Democrats, while Chinese
Americans split roughly between the two parties." Such divergence of
political views shows how Asian ethnic differences are apparent in practice.
(A similar variation of party preference has been observed for Hispanics,
another group which includes large numbers of immigrants and incorporates
several distinct cultures or nationalities; Cuban Americans have tended to
vote strongly Republican, while Puerto Rican and Mexican Americans have
voted mostly for Democrats.[32]) For Asian Americans, cultural differences
and those related to national origin may explain this divergence of opinion,
but it may also reflect a difference of perception formed by the immigrant
experience itself or the length of time most members of the group have been
in the United States.

Political identifications, especially for new participants, may not be
lasting, particularly during a period of emerging Asian political involvement.
Alternately, the party identification chosen by new participants might be
fixed at the outset and grow stronger over time with minimal change in
affiliation. Black voters, for example, switched their allegiance from the
Republican to the Democratic Party in the early part of the century, Jewish

---

[32] Will Mexicans Vote Like Jews or Like Italians. *The Economist, v. 316* September 29, 1990. p.
    23.

voters have consistently favored the Democratic Party, and some white Americans—Catholics, for example—shifted away from earlier Democratic party voting patterns and tend to support Republican candidates in national elections. Political views and party identification could change for a variety of reasons—economic status may change, party allegiance may strengthen or diminish over time, group concerns may shift—and will probably evolve according to the way in which the specific sub-groups of the Asian American community view their relations with the larger society. In a broader sense, the extent to which members of an ethnic group continue to identify with group concerns could have an important effect on their party choice, and how the political parties respond to these perceptions will likely have a strong effect on the formation of party loyalty over time.

VI. REPRESENTATION AMONG ELECTED OFFICIALS

The 103d Congress included eight Asian and Pacific Islanders: two Senators and six Members of the House of Representatives. Three Members were from Hawaii, (including both Members of the Senate), three were from California, and two represented U.S. territories. Only one House Member, Patsy Mink (Hawaii, 2nd district), represented a congressional district that is among the ten with the highest Asian American voting age populations. Historically, there have been 17 Asian American Members of Congress, beginning with Dalip Singh Saund who was elected in 1956 to the 85th Congress.[33]

In State government, Hawaii's Governor John Waihee and Lieutenant Governor Ben Cayetano are the only Asian statewide elected officials aside from the Members of the U.S. Senate mentioned above. Asian American members of state legislatures numbered 54 following the 1992 election: 18 State Senators and 36 Members of State Houses of Representatives.[34] Hawaii accounts for most, with 16 State Senators and 31 State Representatives. If Hawaii is excluded, Asian Americans account for only seven of 7,348 State legislators nationally, or 0.10 percent of the total.

---

[33] U.S. Library of Congress. Congressional Research Service. *Asian Pacific-Americans in the United States Congress*. Report No. 4-767 GOV, by Lorraine H. Tong. Washington, 1994.

[34] These figures were provided by facsimile by the National Conference of State Legislatures, May 1994.

Table 8. Asian American Members of Congress, 1994

Name	State or Territory, District	Chamber	Years of Service
Daniel K. Akaka, D	Hawaii	Senate	1990-present (U.S. House, 1977-1990)
Eni F.H. Faleomavaega, D	American Samoa	House	1989-present
Daniel K. Inouye, D	Hawaii	Senate	1963-present
Jay Kim, R	California, 41st	House	1991-present
Robert T. Matsui, D	California, 5th	House	1979-present
Norman Y. Mineta, D	California, 15th	House	1975-present
Patsy T. Mink, D	Hawaii, 2nd	House	1990-present (U.S. House, 1965-1977)
Robert A. Underwood, D	Guam	House	1993-present

The number of Asian Americans who currently hold local elective office is not available from standard sources. For some areas, however, statistics have been reported on a limited basis. In a 1991 *Los Angeles Times* article, political scientists Roy Christman and James Fay examined Asian American political strength at the local level in California and found a small number of Asian mayors and city council members, representing a fairly large share of the State's population. At that time, there were 40 Asian American mayors or city council members out of 2,419 statewide, or less than 2 percent. Because many of the 40 were elected in the most populous counties of the State, however, they represented 8.9 percent of the population, which is the same percentage of the population that is Asian American.[35]

A study that focused on the election of Asian Americans to city councils in the early 1980s, however, determined that Asian Americans were then underrepresented relative to their share of the population. In cities with populations of 25,000 or more where Asians comprised between 5 to 50 percent of residents, "Asians were underrepresented in the 66 cities by 5.9

---

[35] Christman, Roy, and James Fay. A New Electorate Gains Power. *Los Angeles Times*, November 4, 1991. p. B5.

percentage points."[36] In his analysis of the study's findings, the author pointed out that a city's Asian population does not correlate with city council representation, as it does for blacks. In this respect, Asians are similar to Hispanics since both include large numbers of immigrants and "both contain a fair amount of heterogeneity. Thus, although grouped together as Asians or Hispanics, the differing nationalities comprising each group may not vote in as cohesive a bloc as Blacks."[37]

---

[36] Alozie, Nicholas O. The Election of Asians to City Councils. *Social Science Quarterly*, v. 73, Mar. 1992. p. 92.

[37] Ibid. p. 98.

Chapter 4

ASIAN PACIFIC AMERICAN POLITICAL PARTICIPATION AND REPRESENTATION IN ELECTIVE OFFICE

Kevin Coleman

ABSTRACT

As one of the fastest growing segments of the population, Asian Pacific Americans (APAs) have seemed to be on the verge of greater political activity. As yet the steep increase in the Asian Pacific American population during the last 35 years has not resulted in a corresponding increase in the level of political participation. Voter turnout for Asian Pacific American (APAs) has lagged behind that of whites and blacks, while Asian Pacific American and Hispanic turnout rates are similar (45% for Hispanics in the 2000 election compared with 43% for Asian Pacific Americans).

There are signs of potentially greater political involvement in the future, however. The *Los Angeles Times* reported in a 1997 article that the APA portion of the electorate in California had increased from 3% to 6% between 1992 and 1996, and a 1998 *San Francisco Examiner* city-wide poll found that, despite the high percentage of Asians who are foreign-born, 76% of APAs are citizens compared with 61% of Hispanics.[1] The rapid growth of the APA population is expected to continue into the next century;

---

[1] Gregory Rodriguez, "Southern California Asian Americans May Hold Key to Multiethnic Politics," *Los Angeles Times*, Oct. 5, 1997, p. M1; and Julie Chao, "Despite Gains, City's Asian Americans Still Vote Less, Care Less Than Other Groups," *San Francisco Examiner*, Dec. 6, 1998, p. C1.

whether greater political participation follows will depend on the successful mobilization of the large number of potential voters in the APA community.

Asian immigration to the United States began in the 1840s, and continued throughout the settlement of western and Pacific coast states. Most early immigrants were Chinese laborers whose destinations were the railroads and the mining camps that transformed the western frontier. But restrictive immigration policies and native hostility toward Asian workers (sometimes erupting into riots) followed the settlement period, resulting in self-segregation and the formation of "Chinatowns" in many cities. The adoption of the Chinese Exclusion Act in 1882 (which barred entry to contract laborers for 10 years; 22 Stat. 58) and the Gentlemen's Agreement with Japan in 1908 (whereby Japan agreed to withhold passports from laborers bound for the U.S.) virtually closed off immigration from Asia.

New immigration laws were adopted in 1952 and 1965 that modified earlier restrictions on immigration from Asia. The McCarran-Walter Act of 1952 (66 Stat. 163) eased some restrictions on gaining citizenship and abolished the category called "alien, ineligible for citizenship," which applied to many immigrants from Asia. In 1965, the Immigration and Nationality Act (79 Stat. 911) was amended to eliminate the national quota system and establish new limits of approximately 20,000 immigrants from each Asian country. After that, a renewed flow of immigrants began arriving from Asian countries. Whereas most earlier Asian immigrants arrived from China and Japan, the 1965 changes to immigration laws resulted in a sharp increase in the number of immigrants from India, Korea, the Philippines, Vietnam, and, to a lesser extent, from Cambodia, Laos, Thailand, and Pakistan.

Because the study of Asian Pacific American electoral involvement is a recent phenomenon, little is known about APA political participation historically. Asian immigrants were subject to official and unofficial hostility after they began arriving in the 1840s (anti-Asian immigration laws, discrimination and mob violence, barriers to citizenship, and the internment of Japanese Americans during World War II). Such attitudes may have discouraged political activity. But the social and political dynamic has changed within the Asian Pacific American population, due in part to recent immigration patterns. In 1960, Asian Pacific Americans numbered 900,000 (0.06% of the total population). By 2000, the APA population exceeded eleven million (4.2% of the population), making it one of the fastest-growing populations in the country. Because of this dramatic change in the size and composition of the population, political observers within and outside the APA community anticipate greater political activity.

Table 1. Asian Immigration to the United States, 1971-1990

Place of Origin	1971-1980	1981-1990	Total
China	203,522	474,103	677,625
Hong Kong	47,501	63,016	110,517
Japan	47,914	43,248	91,162
Philippines	360,216	494,971	855,187
Korea	271,463	338,872	610,335
India	176,716	261,841	438,557
Vietnam	178,681	401,419	580,100
Cambodia	8,426	116,571	124,997
Laos	22,566	145,444	168,010
Thailand	44,055	64,437	108,492
Pakistan	31,247	61,364	92,611

Source: Herbert R. Barringer, Robert W. Gardner, and Michael J. Levin, *Asians and Pacific Islanders in the United States* (New York, Russell Sage Foundation, 1993), pp. 25-26.

VOTER TURNOUT

National voter turnout rates for Asian Pacific Americans (APAs) have been available only since 1992, and these data suggest that their participation is lower than that of whites and blacks and similar to Hispanic turnout (see **Table 2**, below). Observers offer a number of reasons to explain the comparatively low rates of voting participation: 1) nearly 70% of Asian Pacific Americans were born outside the U.S., and those who are not yet citizens are not eligible to vote; 2) for some immigrants, a fear or distrust of political involvement carried over from their home countries may inhibit participation; 3) immigrants who do not speak or understand English, or do so only with difficulty, may be discouraged by an "official" activity such as registering and voting; 4) the APA population is comparatively young (APA median age is 30 years compared to a national median of 33 years), and turnout is traditionally lowest among younger voters.[2]

---

[2] U.S. Department of Commerce, Bureau of the Census, *We the Asian Americans*, WE-3, September, 1993. p. 3.

Table 2. Voter Participation Rates in Presidential Elections, 1992 and 1996, by Race and Hispanic Origin

	1992	1996	2000
Asian	27.3%	45.0%	43.3%
White	63.6%	60.7%	61.8%
Hispanic	28.9%	44.3%	45.1%
Black	54.0%	53.0%	56.8%

Source: U.S. Bureau of the Census, "Voting and Registration in the Election of November 1996," [http://www.census.gov/population/www/socdemo/voting.html], visited March 3, 1998, and "Voting and Registration in the Election of November 2000," P20-542, issued February 2002, p.5.

Asian Pacific American voters accounted for one percent of all voters in 1992 and 1996 and two percent of voters in 2000, compared with Hispanics, for example, who accounted for 4% to 7%. In California, APAs were about 5% of the electorate in recent elections, according to exit polls from the *Los Angeles Times*, whereas Hispanics accounted for 8%, 10%, 12%, and 13% of voters, respectively, in statewide elections since 1994.[3] According to a 1998 city-wide poll by the *San Francisco Examiner*, "After several years of intensive organizing, Asian Americans still have the lowest rate of voter registration, voter turnout and general interest in politics of all The City's major racial and ethnic groups."[4]

Despite the potential difficulties immigrants face with respect to voting, a number of factors could work to offset the low rate of participation among APAs. A 1996 national study by the Asian American Studies Center at UCLA found that more than 80% of Asian immigrants become citizens, a step necessary to meet the citizenship requirement for voter registration. A poll of San Francisco's ethnic groups found a similarly high rate of naturalization for APAs (76%), which favorably compared with a 61% naturalization rate for Hispanics in the city.[5] Once registered, APA voters "are among the most likely voters to go to the polls on election day," according to the UCLA study.[6] For example, a study by the Chinese American Voters Education Committee reported that 61% of APA voters

---

[3] Los Angeles Times exit polls, 1994, 1996, and 1998.

[4] Julie Chao, "Despite Gains, City's Asian Americans Still Vote Less, Care Less than Other Groups," p. C1.

[5] Ibid.

[6] Associated Press, Migration News Clip, "Study Tracks Asian Immigrants," available at [http://www.iom.ch/News/c_960327.htm], visited Dec. 10, 1996.

turned out in San Francisco in the November 1996 election, compared with a 59% turnout rate for all voters in the city.[7]

As for language problems with respect to voting, Section 203 of the Voting Rights Act provides that bilingual voting materials are available in certain communities for voters who experience difficulty with English. Section 203 applies to communities where members of a language minority with limited English abilities are 5% of voting age citizens, or the community includes 10,000 members of a language minority who have difficulty with English, and the illiteracy rate for the group exceeds the national illiteracy rate. In California, four counties offer voting materials in one or more languages other than English (Chinese, Japanese, Tagalog, and Vietnamese); in two New York counties and in the borough of Queens, voting materials in Chinese are available; and in Hawaii, voting materials are available in the city and county of Honolulu in Japanese and Tagalog and, in two other counties, in Tagalog only.

VOTING PATTERNS IN ELECTIONS

Partisan voting patterns are mixed for Asian Pacific American voters, according to exit polls for Presidential and U.S. House elections since 1990. Asian Pacific American voters cast 55% of their votes for President Bush in 1992, a plurality (48%) of their votes for Senator Dole in 1996 (Governor Clinton won 31% of the vote in 1992 and, as the incumbent President, won 43% of the vote in 1996), and 62% of their votes for Vice President Gore in 2000. In contrast, APA voters cast a majority of their ballots for Democratic candidates in U.S. House elections in 1990, 1994, and 1998, while a majority voted for Republican candidates in House elections in 1992 and 1996. The results from the 1996 and 1998 House elections illustrate the shifting electoral tendencies of APA voters: a solid majority (56%) voted Republican in 1996 and a slightly higher percentage (57%) voted Democratic in 1998.

Voting patterns in California, where nearly 40% of Asian Pacific Americans live, tend to mirror national voting trends for APAs. According to *Los Angeles Times* exit polls, APA voters cast a majority of their ballots for the Democratic candidate in six of seven elections for U.S. Senator since 1986. In gubernatorial elections, APA voters cast a majority of their votes

---

[7] Ramon G. McLeod, "More Asians Turning Out, Voting in S.F.: Record Levels Contrast With Past Uninvolvement," [http://www.vpac-usa.org/asian/sf_asian.htm], visited April 23, 1998.

for the Democratic candidate three times and for the Republican candidate once.

Table 3. Voting Patterns in Presidential Elections, 1992, 1996, and 2000, by Race and Hispanic Origin

		Asian	White	Black	Hispanic
1992	Clinton (D)	31%	39%	83%	61%
	Bush (R)	55%	40%	10%	25%
	Perot (I)	15%	20%	7%	14%
1996	Clinton (D)	43%	43%	84%	72%
	Dole (R)	48%	46%	12%	21%
	Perot (I)	8%	9%	4%	6%
2000	Bush (R)	37%	54%	9%	38%
	Gore (D)	62%	43%	90%	61%
	Nader	1%	3%	1%	1%

Source: Marjorie Connelly, "Portrait of the Electorate," *The New York Times*, Nov. 10, 1996, p. 28; 2000 data from "The National Electorate," *Los Angeles Times*, Nov. 9, 2000.

Table 4. Asian Pacific American Voting Trends in Senatorial and Gubernatorial Elections in California, 1986-2000

		U.S. Senator		Governor	
Year		Dem	Rep	Dem	Rep
2000		64%	33%	n.a.	n.a.
1998		48%	51%	65%	35%
1994		52%	40%	50%	46%
1992	special election	62%	36%	n.a.	n.a.
	general election	51%	44%	n.a.	n.a.
1990		n.a.	n.a.	52%	44%
1988		51%	47%	n.a.	n.a.
1986		56%	41%	39%	59%

Source: 1998 through 1990 statistics are from various issues of the *Los Angeles Times*: Nov. 3, 1998, Nov. 10, 1994, Nov. 5, 1992, and Nov. 7, 1990; 1988 and 1986 figures are from the Field Institute, Voting in the 1998 General Election, Dec. 1988, and A Survey of 1986 General Election Voters, Dec. 1986.

REPRESENTATION AMONG ELECTED OFFICIALS

The 107th Congress includes nine Asian Pacific Americans: two Senators and seven Members of the House of Representatives. There are three members from Hawaii, two from California, and one each from Oregon and Virginia, as well as one Delegate each from American Samoa and Guam. Historically, there have been 33 APA Members of Congress, beginning with Dalip Singh Saund, who was elected in 1956 to the 85th Congress from California.[8]

**Table 5. Asian Pacific American Members
and Delegates in the 107th Congress**

Name	State	Chamber	Years of service
Daniel Akaka, D	Hawaii	Senate	1990-present (House, 1977-90)
Eni F.H. Faleomavagea, D	American Samoa	House	1989-present
Michael M. Honda, D	California	House	2001-present
Daniel K. Inouye, D	Hawaii	Senate	1963-present
Robert T. Matsui, D	California, 5th	House	1979-present
Patsy T. Mink, D	Hawaii, 2nd	House	1990-present (House, 1965-77)
Robert C. Scott, D[9]	Virginia	House	1993-present
Robert A. Underwood, D	Guam	House	1993-present
David Wu, D	Oregon, 1st	House	1999-present

Source: CRS Report 97-938 GOV, Asian Pacific Americans in the United States Congress, by Lorraine Tong.

At the state level, Gary Locke was elected governor of Washington in 1996, becoming the first Asian Pacific American elected to the office outside Hawaii, and the first Chinese American governor as well. Ben Cayetano

---

[8] This number includes 13 Resident Commissioners from the Philippine Islands who were elected to Congress between 1907 and 1946. For further information, see CRS Report 97-398 GOV, *Asian Pacific Americans in the United States Congress*, by Lorraine Tong.

[9] Rep. Scott is African American with Filipino heritage.

became the first Filipino American state chief executive when he was elected governor of Hawaii in 1994.

Chapter 5

Issues in the Asian-Nation[*]

C.N. Le

PARTICIPATING IN POLITICS

Contrary to what many may assume, Asian Americans are not reluctant to participate in politics. Yen Le Espiritu points out that next to Jews, Asian Americans contribute more money per person to political parties and candidates than any other racial/ethnic or religious group. But as past and recent history shows, that doesn't mean that Asian Americans are always welcomed in the political arena.

Getting into the Arena Early

Even back in the late 1800s, Asians mobilized their resources to lobby for equal rights and access to economic, land, and occupational opportunities that they were being denied. Up through the 1920s, over 1,000 lawsuits were filed in state and federal courts by Asian Americans seeking to receive their proper legal rights. During this time, Asian Americans also organized boycotts, circulated petitions, conducted letter-writing campaigns, published newspapers and magazines promoting their cause, and formed coalitions with several non-Asian organizations.

These activities demonstrate that Asian Americans are not always quiet, modest, and reluctant to "cause trouble." The Asian American community has a clear sense of justice, as illustrated by their collective mobilization to fight for justice regarding Vincent Chin's murder. To that end, many Asian Americans have tried to participate in the political arena, in one form or another.

One of the easiest way to participate is to donate money to candidates or political parties. Such was the case back in 1996 when the Democratic Party was raising funds for President Clinton's reelection. As the nation soon learned, the Democrats were accused of illegally **accepting money from foreigners**. The media and soon Congressional Republicans identified these foreigners as Asian and accused them of trying to influence U.S. policy to the benefit of their Asian countries and businesses. They were accused of trying to "buy" influence with the President.

Thereafter, the Democrats were forced to return a substantial portion of those campaign contributions. Any donor who had an Asian name or who was suspected of having connections to Asian businesses overseas most likely had their contributions returned. Soon after that, Congressional committees began a series of high-profile and public investigations, centering on the now-famous "fundraising" event at a southern California Buddhist temple attended by Al Gore. Ultimately, several Asian Americans entered plea bargains or were convicted of channeling foreign contributions to the Democratic Party.

Stereotypes and Hipocrisy go Hand in Hand

First we should realize that it is legal for permanent residents who are not yet U.S. citizens to donate money. Second, it is legal for U.S. subsidiaries of foreign corporations to donate money if they only donate funds that were earned in the U.S.

Further, anyone can donate if the money goes to a political party rather than an individual politician. Finally, it's interesting why nobody ever accuses Canadian and European corporations of trying to buy influence with the U.S. government, even though their contributions are several times that from Asian companies.

But the most disturbing part of this episode was once again, the entire Asian American community was singled out and publicly vilified for the wrongdoings of just a handful of people. Many politicians and other social commentators were screaming that Asian foreigners were trying to "buy the

White House." Asian Americans were again accused of being deceitful, un-American, and secretly loyal to only Asian countries and businesses.

It is one thing to punish individuals who have actually broken laws. But it is another to then **generalize** suspicions and stereotypes to an entire group of people. All Asian Americans are affected by this prejudice and **racial profiling** -- Republican or Democratic, liberal or conservative. Unfortunately, that was exactly what happened to Asian American in this episode. Sad to say, it will probably not be the last.

The Leaders and Trailblazers

Nonetheless, several Asian Americans past and present have defied these cultural and institutional barriers and have successfully represented not just the Asian American community but their entire multi-racial constituency. The first national Asian American political leaders came from Hawai'i and were able to parlay their broad base of supporters to win seats in the U.S. House of Representative and Senate in the 1950s. The first mainland Asian American to become a member of the U.S. House of Representatives was **Dalip Singh Saund**, a South Asian farmer (with a Ph.D. degree) from central California. The fist mainland Senator was the ultra-conservative **S.I. Hayakawa** from California, former President of San Francisco State University.

More recently, the most prominent Asian American politicians include:

- Senator **Daniel Inouye** of Hawai'i
- Former U.S. Assistant Attorney General for Civil Rights **Bill Lann Lee**
- Governor of the state of Washington **Gary Locke**, the first Asian American governor outside of Hawai'i
- Secretary of Labor **Elaine Chao**
- Secretary of Transportation **Norman Mineta**

Secretary Mineta is the only Democrat serving in President Bush's cabinet and was the first Asian American cabinet Secretary, appointed by former President Clinton to lead the Department of Commerce in 2000.

However, Elaine Chao symbolizes a constant dilemma for the Asian American community. On the one hand, most of us are very proud that she is the first Asian American woman to be a cabinet Secretary. She hopefully represents the growing political power of the Asian American community and a sign that perhaps both political parties will not take us for granted any longer. On the other hand, she's a Republican whereas about **two-thirds** of all Asian Americans who are registered to vote are Democrats.

Therefore, many of us have to weigh the costs and benefits of supporting her as an Asian American versus our dislike for Republican policies and ideology. In the end, as Martin Luther King so eloquently stated, individuals must be judged on the content of their character and what they do -- not on the color of their skin or their ethnicity.

Having said that however, as I have been pointing out throughout this website, we must recognize and appreciate the **diversity** within the Asian American community. This includes differences in terms of ethnicity, age, educational attainment, income, languages and English proficiency, and in this case, political views. In this sense, Secretary Chao, along with Secretary Mineta and all other Asian American politicians serving our country at all levels, deserve our thanks and support.

THE DEMOGRAPHICS OF ASIAN AMERICA

As I mentioned, according to the 2000 U.S. census, Asian Americans make up 4.3% of the total U.S. population -- that's about 12 million people who identify themselves as at least part Asian. However, this number represents an increase of 63% from the 1990 census, making Asian Americans the fastest growing of all the major racial/ethnic groups in the U.S., in terms of percentage growth. But in so many ways, the presence of Asian Americans is much more prominent than even these numbers suggest.

Some Things you May not Have Known

Results from the 2000 Census have given us a detailed picture at how the population of the U.S. has changed in the past few decades, especially in regards to Asian Americans. The Rand Corporation also offers a very good and concise summary of the U.S. population at racial/ethnic demographics. One of their graphics is presented below and it shows the racial/ethnic proportion of the U.S. population from 1900 to projections through 2050.

It shows that in terms of proportion to the total U.S. population, the Black population has stayed and will relatively stable. The groups that are experiencing the highest growth are Hispanics/Latinos and Asian Americans. Conversely, the proportion of the U.S. population who are White is expected to decrease each decade and in 2050, no racial/ethnic group will have be a majority, including Whites for the first time in U.S. history. We can also look at the following table, taken from the 2001 Statistical Abstract of the U.S., published by the Census Bureau. It shows that Asian Americans as a whole are the fastest-growing of all the major racial/ethnic groups, both from 1980-1990 and 1990-2000:

Racial/Ethnic Group	Growth Rate, 1980-1990	Growth Rate, 1990-2000
Whites	4.09%	5.08%
Blacks	11.98%	15.26%
American Indians	35.44%	14.42%
Latinos/Hispanics	53.02%	39.42%
Asian Americans	96.13%	63.24%

However, keep in mind the **first stereotype** about Asian Americans -- that we are all the same. The numbers within the Asian American population show that we are not all alike. This diversity among Asian Americans shows up when we look at the sizes of the different ethnic groups within the overall Asian American population.

This is represented in the following table, compiled using data from the Census Bureau's The Asian Population: Census 2000 Brief. This table includes Asian ethnic groups whose total population is at least 50,000 in size. It breaks down each Asian ethnic group's total population by single ethnicity, two or more Asian ethnicities, and finally, Asian and at least one other race (multiracial Asians).

Ethnic Group	Asian alone		Asian & at least One Other Race (i.e., Filipino-White)	Total Population, Alone or in Any Combination
	Single Ethnicity	Two or More Asian Ethnicities (i.e., Chinese-Vietnamese)		
Chinese	2,314,537	130,826	289,478	2,734,841
Filipino	1,850,314	57,811	456,690	2,364,815
Asian Indian	1,678,765	40,013	180,821	1,899,599
Korean	1,076,872	22,550	129,005	1,228,427
Vietnamese	1,122,528	47,144	54,064	1,223,736
Japanese	796,700	55,537	296,695	1,148,932

Ethnic Group	Asian alone		Asian & at least One Other Race (i.e., Filipino-White)	Total Population, Alone or in Any Combination
Cambodian	171,937	11,832	22,283	206,052
Pakistani	153,533	11,095	39,681	204,309
Laotian	168,707	10,396	19,100	198,203
Hmong	169,428	5,284	11,598	186,310
Thai	112,989	7,929	29,365	150,293
Taiwanese	118,048	14,096	12,651	144,795
Indonesian	39,757	4,429	18,887	63,073
Bangladeshi	41,280	5,625	10,507	57,412

Following up on the total population table and again using data from the 2001 Statistical Abstract of the U.S., it's clear that Chinese are the largest Asian American ethnic group and the following table shows that they comprise 23.7% of the total Asian American population. In terms of growth among the six major Asian American ethnic groups, the Vietnamese were the fastest growing from 1980 to 1990. However, since 1990, Asian Indians have become the fastest growing:

Asian Ethnic Group	Growth Rate 1980-1990	Growth Rate 1990-2000	% of Asian American Popul.
Chinese	104.1%	47.5%	23.7
Filipino	81.6%	30.3%	18.1
Asian Indian	125.6%	113.4%	16.4
Vietnamese	125.3%	89.2%	11.0
Korean	134.8%	35.1%	10.5
Japanese	20.9%	-9.4%	7.8

As you can see, all the Asian ethnic groups listed above grew at a rather healthy rate between 1990 and 2000, except for Japanese Americans. Their population actually declined by almost 10%. Why? Several reasons, actually. First, there are very few Japanese who immigrate to the U.S. these days so therefore they do not experience the type of phenomenal growth that large immigrant groups experience, such as Asian Indians.

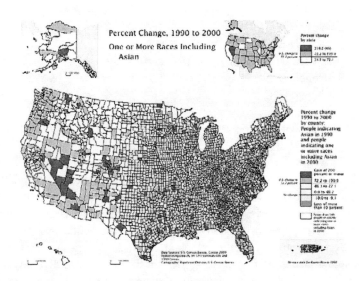

Second, as many Japanese American families are into their fifth or higher generation in the U.S., they have become one of the most assimilated of all Asian American groups. Perhaps as a direct result of this, they also have one of the highest **intermarriage** (interracial marriage) rates of all Asian Americans. As more Japanese Americans intermarry, the less likely their children are to identify themselves as Japanese American.

The map above comes from the "Asian" section of the U.S. Census Bureau's Mapping Census 2000: The Geography of U.S. Diversity report and it illustrates the growth of the Asian American population by county from 1990 to 2000. Click on the thumbnail to see the larger version in a new window. What it basically shows is that the counties that experienced the largest increases in their Asian American population are located in Nevada, Arizona, Colorado, and throughout the south. Keep in mind that this map does not show **absolute** population sizes -- just **increases** in size. In other words, many of the counties that experienced large increases may not have had very many Asian Americans in their counties to begin with.

Data from the 1997-1998 State and Metropolitan Area Data Book, published by the Census Bureau, show that almost **66%** of all Asian Americans live in just **five states**: California (12.1% of the state population), New York (5.6%), Hawai'i (63.6%), Texas (2.9%), and Illinois (3.4%). Amazingly, **54.7%** of all Asian Americans live in just the **six metropolitan areas** below:

Metropolitan Area	Asian American Popul.	% of Total Population
Los Angeles	1,799,000	11.4%
New York	1,343,000	6.7%
San Francisco	1,279,000	18.8%
Honolulu	566,000	64.9%
Washington DC-Baltimore	373,000	5.1%
Chicago	367,000	4.2%

So what's the point to all these statistics? For one, at first glance the Asian American population as a whole may still seem relatively small on a national level. However, in many of the most dynamic and important states and metropolitan areas, our numbers show that we are a **vital and integral** part of that population, culturally, economically, and politically.

Second, while it's useful to look at the Asian American population as a whole, it's also important to recognize that there is a lot of **diversity** among us and between different Asian ethnic groups. Not only are the sizes of the Chinese, Vietnamese, Asian Indian, and other communities different, but they are growing at different rates as well. These differences give each metropolitan area or city its own unique blend of Asian American cultures.

Just as important, different Asian ethnic groups can have very different **socioeconomic** as well as demographic characteristics, which further show that Asian Americans are not all the same.

Chapter 6

THE ASIAN POPULATION: 2000

U.S. Census Bureau

CENSUS 2000 BRIEF

Census 2000 showed that the United States population was 281.4 million on April 1, 2000. Of the total, 11.9 million, or 4.2 percent, reported Asian.[1] This number included 10.2 million people, or 3.6 percent, who reported only Asian and 1.7 million people, or 0.6 percent, who reported Asian as well as one or more other races. Census 2000 asked separate questions on race and Hispanic or Latino origin. Hispanics who reported their race as Asian, either alone or in combination with one or more races, are included in the numbers for Asians.

This report, part of a series that analyzes population and housing data collected from Census 2000, provides a portrait of the Asian population in the United States and discusses its distribution at both the national and subnational levels. It begins by discussing the characteristics of the total Asian population and then focuses on the detailed groups, for example: Asian Indian, Chinese, and Japanese. This report is based on data from the

---

[1] In this report, the term "reported" is used to refer to the answers provided by respondents, as well as responses assigned during the editing and imputation processes. The Asian population includes many groups who differ in language, culture, and length of residence in the United States. Some of the Asian groups, such as the Chinese and Japanese, have been in the United States for several generations. Other groups, such as the Hmong, Vietnamese, Laotians, and Cambodians, are comparatively recent immigrants.

Census 2000 Summary File 1.[2] The text of this report discusses data for the United States, including the 50 states and the District of Columbia.[3]

The term "Asian" refers to people having origins in any of the original peoples of the Far East, Southeast Asia, or the Indian subcontinent (for example, Cambodia, China, India, Japan, Korea, Malaysia, Pakistan, the Philippine Islands, Thailand, and Vietnam). Asian groups are not limited to nationalities, but include ethnic terms, as well.

Figure 1.
Reproduction of the Question on Race From Census 2000

6. What is this person's race? *Mark* ☒ *one or more races* to indicate what this person considers himself/herself to be.

☐ White
☐ Black, African Am., or Negro
☐ American Indian or Alaska Native — *Print name of enrolled or principal tribe.* ↗

☐ Asian Indian   ☐ Japanese   ☐ Native Hawaiian
☐ Chinese   ☐ Korean   ☐ Guamanian or Chamorro
☐ Filipino   ☐ Vietnamese   ☐ Samoan
☐ Other Asian — *Print race.* ↗   ☐ Other Pacific Islander — *Print race.* ↗

☐ Some other race — *Print race.* ↗

Source: U.S. Census Bureau, Census 2000 questionnaire.

The first United States decennial census in 1790 collected data on race, but no distinction was made for people of Asian descent. Data have been collected on the Chinese population since the 1860 census and on the Japanese population since the 1870 census. The racial classification was expanded in the 1910 census to obtain separate figures on other groups such as Filipinos and Koreans. However, data on these other groups were collected on an intermittent basis through the 1970 census. Asian Indians

---

[2] Data from the Census 2000 Summary File 1 were released on a state-by-state basis during the summer of 2001.
[3] Data for the Commonwealth of Puerto Rico are shown in Table 2 and Figure 3.

were classified as White and the Vietnamese population was included in the "Other" race category in the 1970 census.

In the 1980 census, there were six separate response categories for Asians: Asian Indian, Chinese, Filipino, Japanese, Korean, and Vietnamese. These same six categories appeared on both the 1990 and Census 2000 questionnaires. Also, for Census 2000, a separate "Other Asian" response category was added with a write-in area for respondents to indicate specific Asian groups not included on the questionnaire.

THE QUESTION ON RACE WAS CHANGED FOR CENSUS 2000

All U.S. censuses have obtained information on race for every individual, and for the past several censuses, the responses reflect selfidentification. For Census 2000, however, respondents were asked to report *one or more* races they considered themselves and other members of their households to be.[4]

Because of these changes, the Census 2000 data on race are not directly comparable with data from the 1990 census or earlier censuses. Caution must be used when interpreting changes in the racial composition of the United States population over time.

The Census 2000 question on race included 15 separate response categories and 3 areas where respondents could write in a more specific race (see Figure 1). For some purposes, including this report, the response categories and write-in answers were combined to create the five standard Office of Management and Budget race categories, plus the Census Bureau category of "Some other race." The six race categories include:
- White;
- Black or African American;
- American Indian and Alaska
Native;
- Asian;

---

[4] Other changes included terminology and formatting changes, such as spelling out "American" instead of "Amer." for the American Indian or Alaska Native category and adding "Native" to the Hawaiian response category. In the layout of the Census 2000 questionnaire, the seven Asian response categories were alphabetized and grouped together, as were the four Pacific Islander categories after the Native Hawaiian category. The three separate American Indian and Alaska Native identifiers in the 1990 census (i.e., Indian (Amer.), Eskimo, and Aleut) were combined into a single identifier in Census 2000. Also, American Indians and Alaska Natives could report more than one tribe.

• Native Hawaiian and Other
Pacific Islander; and
• Some other race.

For a complete explanation of the race categories used in Census 2000,
see the Census 2000 Brief, *Overview of Race and Hispanic Origin*.[5]

**The Data Collected by Census 2000 on Race can be divided into two
broad Categories: the Race *alone* Population and the Race *in
combination* Population.**

People who responded to the question on race by indicating *only one*
race are referred to as the race *alone* population. For example, respondents
who reported their race as one or more Asian detailed groups, but no other
race, would be included in the Asian *alone* population.[6]

Individuals who reported *more than one* of the six races are referred to
as the race *in combination* population. For example, respondents who
reported they were "Asian *and* Black or African American" or "Asian *and*
White *and* American Indian and Alaska Native"[7] would be included in the
Asian *in combination* population.

**The maximum number of people reporting Asian is reflected in the
Asian *alone or in combination* population.**

One way to define the Asian population is to combine those respondents
who reported only Asian with those who reported Asian as well as one or
more other races. This creates the Asian *alone or in combination* population.
Another way to think of the Asian *alone or in combination* population is the
total number of people who identified entirely or partially as Asian. This
group is also described as people who reported Asian, whether or not they
reported any other races.

---

[5] *Overview of Race and Hispanic Origin: 2000*, U.S. Census Bureau, Census 2000 Brief,
C2KBR/01-1, March 2001, is available on the U.S. Census Bureau's Internet site at
www.census.gov/population/www/cen2000/ briefs.html.

[6] Respondents reporting a single detailed Asian group, such as "Korean" or "Filipino," would be
included in the Asian *alone* population. Respondents reporting more than one detailed
Asian group, such as "Chinese and Japanese" or "Asian Indian and Chinese and
Vietnamese" would also be included in the Asian *alone* population. This is because all of
the detailed groups in these example combinations are part of the larger Asian race
category.

[7] The race in combination categories are denoted by quotations around the combination with the
conjunction *and* in bold and italicized print to indicate the separate races that comprise the
combination.

CENSUS 2000 PROVIDES A SNAPSHOT OF THE ASIAN POPULATION

Table 1 shows the number and percentage of Census 2000 respondents who reported Asian alone as well as those who reported Asian and at least one other race.

Of the total United States population, 10.2 million people, or 3.6 percent, reported only Asian. An additional 1.7 million people reported Asian and at least one other race. Within this group, the most common combinations were "Asian **and** White" (52 percent), followed by "Asian **and** Some other race" (15 percent), "Asian **and** Native Hawaiian and Other Pacific Islander" (8.4 percent) and "Asian **and** Black or African American" (6.4 percent). These four combination categories accounted for 82 percent of all Asians who reported two or more races. Thus, 11.9 million people, or 4.2 percent of the total population, reported Asian alone or in combination with one or more other races.

THE ASIAN POPULATION INCREASED FASTER THAN THE TOTAL POPULATION BETWEEN 1990 AND 2000

Because of the changes made to the question on race in Census 2000, there are at least two ways to present the change in the total number of Asians in the United States. They include: 1) the difference in the Asian population between 1990 and 2000 using the race alone concept for 2000, and 2) the difference in the Asians population between 1990 and 2000 using the race alone or in combination concept for 2000. These comparisons provide a "minimum- maximum" range for the change in the Asian population between 1990 and 2000.

The 1990 census counted 6.9 million Asians. Using the Asian alone population in 2000, this population increased by 3.3 million, or 48 percent, between 1990 and 2000. If the Asian alone or in combination population is used, an increase of 5.0 million, or 72 percent, results. Thus, from 1990 to 2000, the range for the increase in the Asian population was 48 percent to 72 percent. In comparison, the total population grew by 13 percent, from 248.7 million in 1990 to 281.4 million in 2000.

Table 1. Asian Population: 2000

Race	Number	Percent of total population
Total population	**281,421,906**	**100.0**
Asian alone or in combination with one or more other races	11,898,828	4.2
Asian alone	10,242,998	3.6
Asian in combination with one or more other races	1,655,830	0.6
Asian; White	868,395	0.3
Asian; Some other race	249,108	0.1
Asian; Native Hawaiian and Other Pacific Islander	138,802	-
Asian; Black or African American	106,782	-
All other combinations including Asian	292,743	0.1
Not Asian alone or in combination with one or more other races	269,523,078	95.8

- Percentage rounds to 0.0.
Source: U.S. Census Bureau, Census 2000 Summary File1.

THE GEOGRAPHIC DISTRIBUTION
OF THE ASIAN POPULATION

The following discussion of the geographic distribution of the Asian population focuses on the Asian alone or in combination population in the text. As the upper bound of the Asian population, this group includes all respondents who reported Asian, whether or not they reported any other race.[8] Hereafter, in the text of this section, the term "Asian" will be used to refer to those who reported Asian whether they reported one or more than one race. However, in the tables and graphs, data for both the Asian alone and alone or in combination populations are shown.

---

[8] The use of the *alone or in combination* population in this section does not imply that it is the preferred method of presenting or analyzing data. In general, either the *alone* population or the *alone or in combination* population can be used, depending on the purpose of the analysis. The Census Bureau uses both approaches.

About One-Half of the Asian Population Lived in the West[9]

According to Census 2000, of all respondents who reported Asian, 49 percent lived in the West, 20 percent lived in the Northeast, 19 percent lived in the South, and 12 percent lived in the Midwest (see Figure 2).

The West had the highest proportion of Asians in its total population as well as the largest total Asian population: 9.3 percent of all respondents in the West reported Asian, compared with 4.4 percent in the Northeast, 2.3 percent in the South, and 2.2 percent in the Midwest (see Table 2).

Over Half of all People who Reported Asian lived in Just Three States

Over half (51 percent) of the Asian population lived in just three states: California, New York, and Hawaii, which accounted for 19 percent of the total population. California, by far, had the largest Asian population (4.2 million), followed by New York (1.2 million), and Hawaii (0.7 million). The ten states with the largest Asian populations in 2000 were: California, New York, Hawaii, Texas, New Jersey, Illinois, Washington, Florida, Virginia, and Massachusetts (see Table 2). Combined, these states represented 75 percent of the Asian population, but only 47 percent of the total population in the United States.

The Asian population exceeded the U.S. level of 4.2 percent of the total population in nine states. Five states were in the West — Hawaii (58 percent), California (12 percent), Washington (6.7 percent), Nevada (5.6 percent), and Alaska (5.2 percent); two states were in the Northeast — New Jersey and New York (both 6.2 percent); and two states were in the South — Maryland (4.5 percent), and Virginia (4.3 percent). No states in the Midwest had Asian populations greater than the U.S. national average of 4.2 percent.

In nine states, Asians represented less than 1 percent of the total population. Four of those states were located in the South: Alabama,

---

[9] The West region includes the states of Alaska, Arizona, California, Colorado, Hawaii, Idaho, Montana, Nevada, New Mexico, Oregon, Utah, Washington, and Wyoming. The Northeast region includes the states of Connecticut, Maine, Massachusetts, New Hampshire, New Jersey, New York, Pennsylvania, Rhode Island, and Vermont. The South region includes the states of Alabama, Arkansas, Delaware, Florida, Georgia, Kentucky, Louisiana, Maryland, Mississippi, North Carolina, Oklahoma, South Carolina, Tennessee, Texas, Virginia, West Virginia, and the District of Columbia, a state equivalent. The Midwest region includes the states of Illinois, Indiana, Iowa, Kansas, Michigan, Minnesota, Missouri, Nebraska, North Dakota, Ohio, South Dakota, and Wisconsin.

Kentucky, Mississippi, and West Virginia. Two were in the Midwest: North Dakota and South Dakota. Two were in the West: Montana and Wyoming. Maine was the only state in the Northeast with an Asian population less than 1 percent.

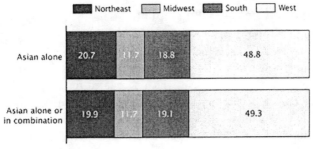

Figure 2.
Percent Distribution of the Asian Population by Region: 2000

(For information on confidentiality protection, nonsampling error, and definitions, see www.census.gov/prod/cen2000/doc/sf1.pdf)

■ Northeast ▢ Midwest ▨ South ▢ West

	Northeast	Midwest	South	West
Asian alone	20.7	11.7	18.8	48.8
Asian alone or in combination	19.9	11.7	19.1	49.3

Source: U.S. Census Bureau, Census 2000 Summary File 1.

The Asian population was concentrated in counties in the West, especially in Hawaii and California.

Of the 3,141 counties in the United States, 122 counties had Asian populations greater than the national average of 4.2 percent, of which 39 counties had at least twice the national average. The overwhelming majority of counties (2,382) had lower concentrations of Asians (less than 1 percent).

Not surprisingly, the counties with the highest concentration of Asians (over 25 percent) were in Hawaii. Honolulu county, by far, had the highest proportion of Asians (62 percent). Three other counties in Hawaii were more than 47 percent Asian, followed by two counties each in Alaska, and the San Francisco Bay area in California.

Table 2. Asian Population for the United States, Regions, and States, and for Puerto Rico: 1990 and 2000

Area	1990			2000							
	Total population	Asian population		Total population	Asian population alone		Asian alone or in combination population		Asian in combination population		
		Number	% of total population		Number	% of total population	Number	% of total population	Number	% of Asian alone or in combination population
United States	248,709,873	6,908,638	2.8	281,421,906	10,242,998	3.6	11,898,828	4.2	1,655,830	13.9
Region										
Northeast	50,809,229	1,324,865	2.6	53,594,378	2,119,426	4.0	2,368,297	4.4	248,871	10.5
Midwest	59,668,632	755,403	1.3	64,392,776	1,197,554	1.9	1,392,938	2.2	195,384	14.0
South	85,445,930	1,094,179	1.3	100,236,820	1,922,407	1.9	2,267,094	2.3	344,687	15.2
West	52,786,082	3,734,191	7.1	63,197,932	5,003,611	7.9	5,870,499	9.3	866,888	14.8
State										
Alabama	4,040,587	21,088	0.5	4,447,100	31,346	0.7	39,458	0.9	8,112	20.6
Alaska	550,043	17,814	3.2	626,932	25,116	4.0	32,686	5.2	7,570	23.2
Arizona	3,665,228	51,699	1.4	5,130,632	92,236	1.8	118,672	2.3	26,436	22.3
Arkansas	2,350,725	12,125	0.5	2,673,400	20,220	0.8	25,401	1.0	5,181	20.4
California	29,760,021	2,735,060	9.2	33,871,648	3,697,513	10.9	4,155,685	12.3	458,172	11.0
Colorado	3,294,394	57,122	1.7	4,301,261	95,213	2.2	120,779	2.8	25,566	21.2
Connec-ticut	3,287,116	50,078	1.5	3,405,565	82,313	2.4	95,368	2.8	13,055	13.7
Delaware	666,168	8,888	1.3	783,600	16,259	2.1	18,944	2.4	2,685	14.2
District of Columbia	606,900	10,923	1.8	572,059	15,189	2.7	17,956	3.1	2,767	15.4

Area	1990			2000						
	Total population	Asian population		Total population	Asian population		Asian alone or in combination population		Asian in combination population	
		Number	% of total population		Number	% of total population alone	Number	% of total population	Number	% of Asian alone or in combination population
Florida	12,937,926	149,856	1.2	15,982,378	266,256	1.7	333,013	2.1	66,757	20.0
Georgia	6,478,216	73,764	1.1	8,186,453	173,170	2.1	199,812	2.4	26,642	13.3
Hawaii	1,108,229	522,967	47.2	1,211,537	503,868	41.6	703,232	58.0	199,364	28.3
Idaho	1,006,749	8,492	0.8	1,293,953	11,889	0.9	17,390	1.3	5,501	31.6
Illinois	11,430,602	282,569	2.5	12,419,293	423,603	3.4	473,649	3.8	50,046	10.6
Indiana	5,544,159	36,660	0.7	6,080,485	59,126	1.0	72,839	1.2	13,713	18.8
Iowa	2,776,755	25,037	0.9	2,926,324	36,635	1.3	43,119	1.5	6,484	15.0
Kansas	2,477,574	30,708	1.2	2,688,418	46,806	1.7	56,049	2.1	9,243	16.5
Kentucky	3,685,296	16,983	0.5	4,041,769	29,744	0.7	37,062	0.9	7,318	19.7
Louisiana	4,219,973	40,173	1.0	4,468,976	54,758	1.2	64,350	1.4	9,592	14.9
Maine	1,227,928	6,450	0.5	1,274,923	9,111	0.7	11,827	0.9	2,716	23.0
Maryland	4,781,468	138,148	2.9	5,296,486	210,929	4.0	238,408	4.5	27,479	11.5
Massachusetts	6,016,425	142,137	2.4	6,349,097	238,124	3.8	264,814	4.2	26,690	10.1
Michigan	9,295,297	103,501	1.1	9,938,444	176,510	1.8	208,329	2.1	31,819	15.3
Minnesota	4,375,099	76,952	1.8	4,919,479	141,968	2.9	162,414	3.3	20,446	12.6
Mississippi	2,573,216	12,679	0.5	2,844,658	18,626	0.7	23,281	0.8	4,655	20.0
Missouri	5,117,073	39,271	0.8	5,595,211	61,595	1.1	76,210	1.4	14,615	19.2
Montana	799,065	3,958	0.5	902,195	4,691	0.5	7,101	0.8	2,410	33.9
Nebraska	1,578,385	11,945	0.8	1,711,263	21,931	1.3	26,809	1.6	4,878	18.2
Nevada	1,201,833	35,232	2.9	1,998,257	90,266	4.5	112,456	5.6	22,190	19.7

Area	1990			2000						
	Total population	Asian population		Total population	Asian population		Asian alone or in combination population		Asian in combination population	
		Number	% of total population		Number	alone % of total population	Number	% of total population	Number	% of Asian alone or in combination population
New Hampshire	1,109,252	9,121	0.8	1,235,786	15,931	1.3	19,219	1.6	3,288	17.1
New Jersey	7,730,188	270,839	3.5	8,414,350	480,276	5.7	524,356	6.2	44,080	8.4
New Mexico	1,515,069	13,363	0.9	1,819,046	19,255	1.1	26,619	1.5	7,364	27.7
New York	17,990,455	689,303	3.8	18,976,457	1,044,976	5.5	1,169,200	6.2	124,224	10.6
North Carolina	6,628,637	49,970	0.8	8,049,313	113,689	1.4	136,212	1.7	22,523	16.5
North Dakota	638,800	3,317	0.5	642,200	3,606	0.6	4,967	0.8	1,361	27.4
Ohio	10,847,115	89,723	0.8	11,353,140	132,633	1.2	159,776	1.4	27,143	17.0
Oklahoma	3,145,585	32,002	1.0	3,450,654	46,767	1.4	58,723	1.7	11,956	20.4
Oregon	2,842,321	64,232	2.3	3,421,399	101,350	3.0	127,339	3.7	25,989	20.4
Pennsylvania	11,881,643	135,784	1.1	12,281,054	219,813	1.8	248,601	2.0	28,788	11.6
Rhode Island	1,003,464	18,019	1.8	1,048,319	23,665	2.3	28,290	2.7	4,625	16.3
South Carolina	3,486,703	21,399	0.6	4,012,012	36,014	0.9	44,931	1.1	8,917	19.8

Area	1990			2000						
	Total population	Asian population		Total population	Asian population	alone	Asian alone or in combination population		Asian in combination population	
		Number	% of total population		Number	% of total population	Number	% of total population	Number	% of Asian alone or in combination population
South Dakota	696,004	2,938	04	754,844	4,378	0.6	6,009	0.8	1,631	27.1
Tennessee	4,877,185	30,944	0.6	5,689,283	56,662	1.0	68,919	1.2	12,257	17.8
Texas	16,986,510	311,918	1.8	20,851,820	562,319	2.7	644,193	3.1	81,874	12.7
Utah	1,722,850	25,696	1.5	2,233,169	37,108	1.7	48,692	2.2	11,584	23.8
Vermont	562,758	3,134	0.6	608,827	5,217	0.9	6,622	1.1	1,405	21.2
Virginia	6,187,358	156,036	2.5	7,078,515	261,025	3.7	304,559	4.3	43,534	14.3
Washington	4,866,692	195,918	4.0	5,894,121	322,335	5.5	395,741	6.7	73,406	18.5
West Virginia, 793,477	7,283	0.4	1,808, 344	9,434	0.5	11,873	0.7	2,439	20.5	
Wisconsin	4,891,769	52,782	1.1	5,363,675	88,763	1.7	102,768	1.9	14,005	13.6
Wyoming	453,588	2,638	0.6	493,782	2,771	0.6	4,107	0.8	1,336	32.5
Puerto Rico	**3,522,037**	**(X)**	**(X)**	**3,808,610**	**7,960**	**0.2**	**17,279**	**0.5**	**9,319**	**53.9**

X Not applicable.
Source: U.S. Census Bureau, Census 2000 Summary File 1; 1990 Census of Population, General Population Characteristics (1990 CP-1).

Although Asians resided in an array of counties, the largest concentrations tended to be found in coastal and/or urban counties, while smaller concentrations were scattered throughout the United States (see Figure 3). The majority of the counties with Asian populations more than twice the national average were predominately concentrated in suburbs of large metropolitan areas such as Seattle, Washington; Los Angeles and the San Francisco Bay area of California; New York, New York; Newark, New Jersey; Washington, DC; Chicago, Illinois; Houston, Texas; and the Minneapolis-St.Paul, Minnesota, metropolitan area. Concentrations of Asians outside the suburbs of large metropolitan areas were typically located near colleges and universities.

Los Angeles county was the only county with over one million Asians. Honolulu county was the only other county with an Asian population over one-half million.

The Asian population was concentrated in counties in the West, especially in Hawaii and California.

Of the 3,141 counties in the United States, 122 counties had Asian populations greater than the national average of 4.2 percent, of which 39 counties had at least twice the national average. The overwhelming majority of counties (2,382) had lower concentrations of Asians (less than 1 percent).

Not surprisingly, the counties with the highest concentration of Asians (over 25 percent) were in Hawaii. Honolulu county, by far, had the highest proportion of Asians (62 percent). Three other counties in Hawaii were more than 47 percent Asian, followed by two counties each in Alaska, and the San Francisco Bay area in California.

Although Asians resided in an array of counties, the largest concentrations tended to be found in coastal and/or urban counties, while smaller concentrations were scattered throughout the United States (see Figure 3). The majority of the counties with Asian populations more than twice the national average were predominately concentrated in suburbs of large metropolitan areas such as Seattle, Washington; Los Angeles and the San Francisco Bay area of California; New York, New York; Newark, New Jersey; Washington, DC; Chicago, Illinois; Houston, Texas; and the Minneapolis-St.Paul, Minnesota, metropolitan area. Concentrations of Asians outside the suburbs of large metropolitan areas were typically located near colleges and universities.

Los Angeles county was the only county with over one million Asians. Honolulu county was the only other county with an Asian population over one-half million.

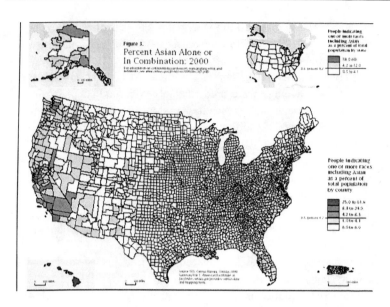

Figure 3.
Percent Asian Alone or
In Combination: 2000

The two places with the largest Asian populations were New York and Los Angeles.[1]

Census 2000 showed that, of all places in the United States with 100,000 or more population, New York had the largest Asian population with 872,777, followed by Los Angeles with 407,444 (see Table 3). Eight places had Asian populations over 100,000: five in the West, and one each in the Northeast, Midwest, and the South.

Of the ten largest places in the United States, San Diego had the largest proportion of Asians (15 percent), followed by Los Angeles and New York with 11 percent each. Asians represented 1.3 percent of the total population in Detroit, the lowest percentage among the country's ten largest cities.

---

[1] Census 2000 showed 245 places in the United States with 100,000 or more population. They included 238 incorporated places (including 4 city-county consolidations) and 7 census designated places that were not legally incorporated. For a list of these places by state, see *www.census.gov/population/www/cen2000/ phc-t6.html*.

ADDITIONAL FINDINGS ON THE ASIAN POPULATION

Which Asian Group was the Largest?

According to Census 2000, Chinese was the largest detailed Asian group in the United States. This is true for both the alone and the alone or in combination populations. There were 2.3 million people who reported only Chinese and an additional 0.4 million people who reported Chinese with at least one other race or Asian group. A total of 2.7 million people reported Chinese alone or in combination with one or more other races or Asian groups (see Table 4).

Filipinos and Asian Indians were the next two largest specified Asian groups. There were 1.9 million people who reported Filipino alone and an additional 0.5 million who reported Filipino in combination with one or more other races or Asian groups. This gives a total of 2.4 million people who reported Filipino alone or in combination with at least one other race or Asian group. About 1.7 million people reported only Asian Indian and an additional 0.2 million reported Asian Indian in combination with one or more other races or Asian groups. A total of 1.9 million people reported Asian Indian alone or in combination with at least one other race or Asian group.

Combined, Chinese, Filipinos, and Asian Indians accounted for 58 percent of all respondents who reported a single Asian group. Of all Asian groups mentioned in race combinations, these three groups accounted for 57 percent of all responses.

Among the largest Asian groups, which was most likely to be in combination with one or more other races or Asian groups?

Of the six largest specified Asian groups, Japanese were most likely to report one or more other races or Asian groups. Of all respondents who reported Japanese, either alone or in combination, 31 percent reported one or more other races or Asian groups (see Figure 5). This included 4.8 percent who reported Japanese with one or more other Asian groups, 21 percent who reported Japanese with one or more other races, and 4.8 percent who reported Japanese in addition to one or more other races and Asian groups (see Table 4). Vietnamese were least likely to be in combination with one or more other races or Asian groups. Of all respondents who reported Vietnamese, 8.3 percent reported one or more other races or Asian groups.

Table 4. Asian Population by Detailed Group: 2000

Detailed group	Asian alones		Asian in combination with one or more other races		Asian detailed group alone or in any combination[2]
	One Asian group reported[1]	Two or more Asian groups reported[2]	One Asian group reported	Two or more Asian groups reported[2]	
Total	**10,019,405**	**223,593**	**1,516,841**	**138,989**	**11,898,828**
Asian Indian	1,678,765	40,013	165,437	15,384	1,899,599
Bangladeshi	41,280	5,625	9,655	852	57,412
Bhutanese	183	9	17	3	212
Burmese	13,159	1,461	1,837	263	16,720
Cambodian	171,937	11,832	20,830	1,453	206,052
Chinese, except Taiwanese	2,314,537	130,826	201,688	87,790	2,734,841
Filipino	1,850,314	57,811	385,236	71,454	2,364,815
Hmong	169,428	5,284	11,153	445	186,310
Indo Chinese	113	55	23	8	199
Indonesian	39,757	4,429	17,256	1,631	63,073
Iwo Jiman	15	3	60	-	78
Japanese	796,700	55,537	241,209	55,486	1,148,932
Korean	1,076,872	22,550	114,211	14,794	1,228,427
Laotian	168,707	10,396	17,914	1,186	198,203
Malaysian	10,690	4,339	2,837	700	18,566
Maldivian	27	2	22	-	51
Nepalese	7,858	351	1,128	62	9,399
Okinawan	3,513	2,625	2,816	1,645	10,599
Pakistani	153,533	11,095	37,587	2,094	204,309
Singaporean	1,437	580	307	70	2,394
Sri Lankan	20,145	1,219	2,966	257	24,587
Taiwanese	118,048	14,096	11,394	1,257	144,795
Thai	112,989	7,929	27,170	2,195	150,283
Vietnamese	1,122,528	47,144	48,639	5,425	1,223,736
Other Asian, not specified3	146,870	19,576	195,449	7,535	369,430

- Represents zero.

1The total of 10,019,405 respondents categorized as reporting only one Asian group in this table is lower than the total of 10,019,410 shown in Table PCT5 (U.S. Census Bureau, Census 2000 Summary File 1 100-Percent Data, see *factfinder.census.gov*). This table includes more detailed groups than PCT5. This means that, for example, an individual who reported "Pakistani *and* Nepalese" is shown in this table as reporting two or more Asian groups. However, that same individual is categorized as reporting a single Asian group in PCT5 because both Pakistani and Nepalese are part of the larger Other specified Asian group.

2The numbers by detailed Asian group do not add to the total population. This is because the detailed Asian groups are tallies of the number of Asian *responses* rather than the number of Asian *respondents*. Respondents reporting several Asian groups are counted several times. For example, a respondent reporting "Korean *and* Filipino" would be included in the Korean as well as the Filipino numbers.

3Includes respondents who checked the "Other Asian" response category on the census questionnaire or wrote in a generic term such as "Asian" or "Asiatic."

Source: U.S. Census Bureau, Census 2000, special tabulations.

Figure 5.

Percent Distribution of Selected Detailed Asian Groups by Alone or in Combination Population: 2000

(For information on confidentiality protection, nonsampling error, and definitions, see *www.census.gov/prod/cen2000/doc/sf1.pdf*)

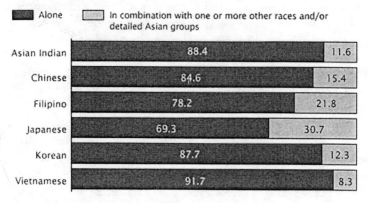

| ■ Alone | ☐ In combination with one or more other races and/or detailed Asian groups |

	Alone	In combination
Asian Indian	88.4	11.6
Chinese	84.6	15.4
Filipino	78.2	21.8
Japanese	69.3	30.7
Korean	87.7	12.3
Vietnamese	91.7	8.3

Source: U.S. Census Bureau, Census 2000, special tabulations.

Were there differences in median age between the Asian alone and the Asian in combination populations and the total U.S. population?

The median age of the total U.S. population was 35.3 years. The overall median age for people who reported Asian alone was 32.7 years, which was 2.6 years younger than the total population. Those who reported Asian in combination with one or more races had a median age of 31.1 years, which was 4.2 years younger than the total.

ABOUT CENSUS 2000

Why did Census 2000 ask The question on Race?

The Census Bureau collects data on race to fulfill a variety of legislative and program requirements. Data on race are used in the legislative redistricting process carried out by the states and in monitoring local jurisdictions' compliance with the Voting Rights Act. These data are also essential for evaluating federal programs that promote equal access to employment, education, and housing and for assessing racial disparities in health and exposure to environmental risks. More broadly, data on race are critical for research that underlies many policy decisions at all levels of government.

How do data from the question on race benefit me, my family, and my community?

All levels of government need information on race to implement and evaluate programs, or enforce laws. Examples include: the Native American Programs Act, the Equal Employment Opportunity Act, the Civil Rights Act, the Voting Rights Act, the Public Health Act, the Healthcare Improvement Act, the Job Partnership Training Act, the Equal Credit Opportunity Act, the Fair Housing Act, and the Census Redistricting Data Program.

Both public and private organizations use race information to find areas where groups may need special services and to plan and implement education, housing, health, and other programs that address these needs. For example, a school system might use this information to design cultural activities that reflect the diversity in their community. Or a business could use it to select the mix of merchandise it will sell in a new store. Census information also helps identify areas where residents might need services of particular importance to certain racial or ethnic groups, such as screening for hypertension or diabetes.

INDEX